Who Do You
Think You Are?

Who Do You Think You Are?

AN INTERACTIVE JOURNEY THROUGH YOUR PAST LIVES AND INTO YOUR BEST FUTURE

Michelle Brock

A TarcherPerigee Book

an imprint of Penguin Random House LLC
penguinrandomhouse.com

Interior art: Modern thin line icons © DStarky / shutterstock.com;
Vector exercise yoga icon © MAKSIM ANKUDA / shutterstock.com

TarcherPerigee with tp colophon is a registered trademark
of Penguin Random House LLC.

Most TarcherPerigee books are available at special quantity discounts for bulk
purchase for sales promotions, premiums, fund-raising, and educational needs.
Special books or book excerpts also can be created to fit specific needs.
For details, write SpecialMarkets@penguinrandomhouse.com.

Library of Congress Cataloging-in-Publication Data

Names: Brock, Michelle, author.
Title: Who do you think you are?: an interactive journey through your
past lives and into your best future / Michelle Brock.
Description: [New York]: TarcherPerigee, [2024]
Identifiers: LCCN 2023025055 (print) | LCCN 2023025056 (ebook) |
ISBN 9780593543559 (trade paperback) | ISBN 9780593543566 (epub)
Subjects: LCSH: Reincarnation therapy—Popular works. |
Self-actualization (Psychology)
Classification: LCC RC489.R43 B76 2024 (print) | LCC RC489.R43 (ebook) |
DDC 616.89/14—dc23/eng/20231016
LC record available at https://lccn.loc.gov/2023025055
LC ebook record available at https://lccn.loc.gov/2023025056

Printed in the United States of America
1st Printing

Book design by Laura K. Corless

For Skyler and Jesse, my two greatest teachers

contents

SECTION I
HONOR THE PAST

introduction

We have all been here before.

What I mean is, we have all lived in other forms, other bodies, other places, and other times. Yes, I am talking about reincarnation.

Reincarnation—the concept that we all have a past that took place in other lifetimes—is something I have come to believe in. I didn't grow up with this idea. In fact, I was raised in a tradition that completely shunned such notions.

But I came to reincarnation the most powerful way: through my own experience.

Past lives can be remembered and experienced. I have recalled my own past lives, and the details have revealed that I have been different races, ethnicities, religions, and even genders than I am today.

Over the years, I have also helped guide thousands of individuals into the experience of their past. I have worked with people of all backgrounds and beliefs, and many elements to the journey of the soul through its lifetimes seem to be universal or, dare I say, human.

Our past lives are not ancient, ethereal, or far away, with nothing to do with now. Rather, they are a part of us. In fact, our past lives make up exactly who we are today. They live inside our unconscious mind, impacting our choices, preferences, and emotional states. They create our fears. They rule our negative thought patterns and the formation of our limiting belief systems.

Uncovering your past lives is a matter of learning how to navigate the often-stormy waters of the mind. Your past lives are there, right under the surface. Accessing them is only a matter of knowing where to look.

This book will act as a guide to locating those past lives, and to finding the memories of who you were before.

But then what? After you learn the story of your own past, how do you apply that knowledge to your life *here*, the one you are living right now?

Although history is interesting, I believe that what matters most is this life, right now, and the future we are creating. If we have already grown old and wise many times, how can we use that wisdom to navigate our lives today?

This book will show you how to use your past lives as a tool to discover your true identity, the one that has nothing to do with the body you are in right now or the life you are currently living. This new identity, as a soul and not a body, can help you find peace in the present moment, change how you look at yourself and others, and construct a new future for yourself that is free of your past.

You read that right.

You are creating the future. I want you to know that what lies ahead has not yet been determined. It is true that certain things will happen, or are "meant to be," but the path ahead of you has not been forged. You are actively creating this future with each and every thought, word, and action. It is my belief that there is no such thing as fate but, instead, a principle called destiny.

Fate is something we can look at only in hindsight, but destiny requires action. Destiny also contains a spiritual dimension. We hear phrases like "stepping into your destiny," which means a courage is gathered or a faith is found in order to take that leap. It means an action is taken that represents another step forward in your evolution, toward your purpose.

This is not just your life's purpose, by the way. Your destiny is your soul's purpose. By clearing anything from your past that is holding you back, and understanding more about who you truly are, you can step into this divine purpose and the future that reflects your highest destiny. This future will reflect your newfound wisdom, healing, and understanding and bring you all the happiness, love, and joy you could ever possibly find in this lifetime.

I also want to be clear that in my current life as a white woman living in a major urban center within a white supremacist society, I would never lay claim to someone else's identity in the here and now. One goal of past lives work is to increase our empathy by unearthing our shared human identity, which means being open to hearing the experiences of others, even when it is painful. Listen. Hold space. Stay sensitive; stay compassionate.

We can all work together to change the future for the collective, too, in our communities, in our countries, and across the planet. Discovering your true identity by way of understanding your past lives can help make a shift that will bring about a new future for all of humanity.

May this book be of service to you, to your families, to all the lives you touch, and to all beings everywhere.

With love,
Michelle Brock

how to use this book

My intention in writing this book is to give you, my dear reader, a chance to experience your past lives—but first I want to share some important things to know about this process:

* Everyone experiences past-life memories in their own way.

* You may see yourself quite clearly in vivid detail, or you may perceive only quick impressions.

* Some people do not "see" anything but have an inner "knowing" or feeling of what is occurring.

* Others describe the experience as though someone is telling them what is happening or narrating a scene.

* It is necessary to focus on all of your senses while doing any past-life exercise because you may be surprised which are specific to you.

* Strong emotions, smells, sounds, temperature differences, and textures are all part of the experience.

* It is not uncommon for someone who is discovering a past life for the first time to feel as if all or part of the experience may have been imagined.

* Sometimes a person will question the source of the material, believing that it may have come from a movie they have seen or some other place or event.

* It is crucial to know that the subconscious mind often works with symbols, a phenomenon that we are most familiar with through our dreams.

* Remember to keep an open mind and to not actively analyze your experience while you're in it.

* You will get more out of the process if you give yourself over as it unfolds. There will be plenty of time for analysis and interpretation afterward.

* Certain memories or images experienced during past-life regression may represent traumatic events, which can evoke intense emotional reactions or distress.

* These emotionally charged images are often useful for facilitating insight, understanding, and healing, but nonetheless, they can be emotionally troubling.

* Uncovering past-life memories is not something that should be entered into lightly and should be done by someone who is grounded and ready to deal with any issues that may arise. Ideally, you are someone who has a healthy sense of self from this life and are not struggling with any mental health conditions or symptoms that could inadvertently become exacerbated through this process. If in doubt, please consult a qualified professional before embarking on this journey.

* Accessing past-life memories is an entirely voluntary experience.

* If at any time the experience becomes too uncomfortable or you feel unwilling to proceed, you may simply open your eyes and the process will stop.

* Many people do not experience memories from their past lives right away; it takes practice over time. If this is true for you, do not be discouraged! Walk away and try again another time.

* Many factors can influence a person's ability to experience past-life memories, including individual capacity for relaxation and imagination; being tired, hungry, or distracted; or putting too much pressure on themselves to have the experience.

* I encourage you to relax as much as you can and don't be hard on yourself if it doesn't happen the first time.

* Keep trying, and allow this process to unfold in its own way and time.

SECTION I

Honor the Past

one

YOU ARE NOT
YOUR NAME

Imagine you are attending an enormous conference, held in a gigantic room like a hotel ballroom, and hundreds of people are lined up to enter. As you get to the door, you see a table with a bunch of markers and name tags that read, "Hello: My Name Is _____."

Before you enter the room full of strangers, you write your name on a tag, allowing you to identify yourself to potential friends or colleagues without having to say a word. How relieved are you that you can wear that name tag? How glad are you that you can easily read the names of the others at this conference before you begin a conversation?

By writing down your name, you have claimed your identity and displayed it, giving yourself a human presence among the crowd.

Our name is the first way we create an identity. It begins at birth, or even before, while our parents are imagining us and who we might become. In many ways, the process of thinking of a name for an unborn baby makes it real—the fact that you are about to create and raise a human being.

This is true whether a baby is planned or unplanned. A child is born into this life and given a name. Even though we have lived many times before, our name is often what first gives us our humanity. Because you have lived before, in past lives, you have had different names in other times, in other places, and in other bodies. And when you died, you left behind that name, along with that body, to continue on with your journey into your next life.

But when you were alive in that past life, your name was the way you connected to your own sense of self, or your identity, just as it is now. Names reflect background and culture and the way parents and family want their children to be seen. They are often a direct line to your ancestors, perhaps once belonging to a beloved grandparent, aunt, or other family member, chosen to be revered in this new child. Some people even have the same name as their father or grandfather and are referred to as "junior" or "the third."

Different cultures around the world have unique traditions around names. In China, it is the custom to have the surname (or family name) come first, before the given name of the individual. In Spain and Latin America, babies are often given two surnames, one from the father and one from the mother. This practice ensures that the mother's family's name will continue to live on in the child (and makes for some very long names!).

Many names contain a reference to a specific culture, helping maintain an identity within a tribe, group, or ethnicity. In South Africa, the Zulu often give a child a name that represents the circumstances around when or where they were born, such as the place of birth, what was happening in the tribe or family at that time, or the day of the week. These Zulu names can include the intentions or wishes the parents have for the child, their life, and their expected place in the community.

Names often hold definitions or meanings, and many expectant parents spend time poring over baby name books, looking for just the right one to set the tone for the life of their child.

Think for a moment about how you got your name, if you know the story. If you don't know it and have a parent or family member whom you can ask, I encourage you to have that conversation.

What was the inspiration for your name? What is the meaning of your name?

Take a minute to think about your own feelings in connection to your name. Do you like your name? Can you easily identify with it? It is not uncommon for people to either change their name to something they feel is more in alignment with who they are, or use a middle name or a nickname instead. Ask yourself if your name represents who you are, right now, in your current lifetime.

Naming a child after a positive association—an idea that can translate into feelings of positivity about themselves or their path in life—is something nearly every culture on Earth does. I named both of my children based on my own positive associations with their monikers and chose names with meanings that I felt would set them both on a path toward happiness and success.

Many names come from nature, inspired by flowers, trees,

JOURNAL TIME

As you work through this book, consider keeping a journal to record your thoughts. This journal can be in whatever form you're most comfortable using—handwriting in a notebook, typing in a word-processing file, or recording observations in your phone's Notes or Voice Memos app, for example.

Ask yourself:

What does your name mean? (If you don't know, you can look it up!)

Do you identify with your name and its meaning? How? And how not?

Why did your parents choose to give you that particular name?

How do you feel your name has influenced your journey through your life so far?

Is there anything about your name you would change or add to?

and herbs. Others are chosen because they describe desirable qualities, such as strength, integrity, or faith, with the wish that the child will take on those characteristics.

In many religious traditions, parents choose a name that represents a saint or religious figure in the hopes that the child will emulate them and even receive their guidance and protection. This is why names like Mary, Joseph, Joshua, Moses, Jesus, and Mohammed are so common.

Names are often considered sacred, and the act of giving a child a name is sometimes marked by a ceremony or ritual. In Jewish tradition, a baby is given a Hebrew name in a formal ceremony attended by family and friends. The belief around this ceremony is that the baby's soul is not fully attached to the body until the name is given. Only then does that child's soul commit to that body to live its life. The name represents the life the child's parents intend for them. For boys, this naming ceremony is performed eight days after birth; for girls, there is no specified time, but it is usually done in the first weeks of life.

Islamic tradition has a sacred naming tradition, too, usually performed on the seventh day of life. In Japan, baby naming also happens on the seventh day, when the father writes the name and date of birth on a piece of paper and posts it for everyone to see. In the Gambia and Senegal, naming is celebrated with a big feast, during which the spiritual leader or tribal elder repeatedly whispers the name into the baby's ear. This takes place the eighth day after birth.

Several Native American traditions view names as fluid, able to be changed at any time. This is an acknowledgment of the idea that a person's name is an embodiment of their potential, or the trajectory of their journey, which can change as a person grows and evolves. For example, if a tribal member overcomes something difficult or achieves something great, they may earn a new name that describes this new version of themselves. This tradition inspires each individual to look toward who they are becoming in the future, rather than bearing the name of an ancestor and carrying the weight of the past. I love this idea because we are all continually evolving and growing.

REVISIONIST HISTORY

In many cultures, it is customary to change one's name, at least in part, after a significant life event, reflecting the idea that certain situations can alter the nature or character of an individual. For example, many people change their names after getting married, going through a divorce, or being widowed. Or it may be after coming of age, experiencing a rite of passage, or completing an achievement in one's life.

In certain Jewish communities, if someone becomes very ill, the family might change their name, hoping that doing so will inspire the person's condition to improve. In China, a child's name is sometimes changed to improve their luck in life.

What are some of the pivotal moments in your life so far that have transformed you in some profound way? What (if any) new name would you give yourself connected to this turning point? How does this new name reflect the person you have become after this event?

I have heard many people share special stories about how they chose a name for their child. These accounts include seeing or encountering something unique and unexpected, such as an animal or a stone. One mother, while on a walk in the woods, found what she thought was glass but later proved to be a piece of amber. She considered that a special moment because it seemed like something she was meant to find. When her daughter was born, she named her Amber.

I've also heard stories from expectant parents who claim that they received their child's name in a dream. Many cultures believe that when a woman is pregnant, particularly when the time of birth is near, the veil between the physical world and the world of spirit is thin. A mother-to-be may be able to touch other dimensions of reality and, therefore, is more open to receiving messages from divine sources, including being "gifted" a name.

We assign names to our loved ones as terms of endearment, or ways we show affection to those with whom we are close. Nicknames that come about after an event, a shared memory, or even an inside joke solidify and maintain strong bonds between people. I have several nicknames for both of my children, ones that usually make them laugh or feel loved when I use them. Terms like *honey*, *baby*, *darling*, *dear*, or *love* are usually reserved for the closest people to you. (I don't recommend addressing a stranger as "Hey, baby.")

My point is that names, and how we use them, matter. Our names are how we connect to ourselves and interact with each other. A name is much more than what you are called.

Your name is a source of personal empowerment. It is how you identify yourself. It is the "I am" answer to the question "Who are you?" Even though our existence does not begin or end in this life, and we have many lifetimes in many different forms, your name in *this* life is how you relate to your sense of self right now.

Most people enjoy hearing their name because it makes them feel seen, recognized, and validated. This is why successful salespeople and customer service professionals understand the power of using someone's name. It allows that person to feel as if they are being approached as a human being and not a number, case file, or demographic.

It works the other way, too. If you mispronounce or forget someone's name, that is the fastest way to make them feel as if you don't care about them. In fact, a tactic used throughout history to strip away a person's strength and connection to their humanity has been to take away their name. During chattel slavery in the United States, one of the largest crimes against humanity in all of history, many enslaved Africans and African Americans were recorded only by their gender and age in order to dehumanize them. Slave ledgers, which were the official records of the people an owner enslaved, generally did not include the person's given name, just age and gender or perhaps the last name of their enslaver. As a result, it is nearly impossible for African Americans to trace their ancestry to any time before the Civil War. By omitting their names, slave traders and owners found it easier not to see the enslaved as human beings with feelings, hopes, wishes, and dreams.

This dehumanization also happens when you force someone to change their name, such as when Christian names were forced upon Native American children who had been taken from their families, well into the twentieth century. During the Holocaust, inmates at certain death camps were assigned numbers and not called by their names. When a person is made nameless, it is easier to pretend they aren't worthy of the same humanity as one whose name we know and speak. In fact, many memorials are simple but powerful lists of names, such as the Vietnam Veterans Memorial in Washington, DC, and the New England Holocaust Memorial in Boston.

One of the most incredible places I have ever been is the Temple of Apollo on Mount Parnassus in Greece. This structure was considered a sacred site for hundreds of years. It was the home of the Pythia, one of the most famous Oracles, or psychics, of the ancient world, and it has been featured in works by Plutarch, Ovid, Sophocles, Plato, and Aristotle. It was also the place you would visit when you wanted to free a slave. A slave became free after their master inscribed their name on the stone at the base of the temple. That action not only was symbolically weighted but also forged a permanent record that proved the named person was indeed free.

The characters and letters that make up the thousands of names etched in the stone there are still visible. Each name represents a person whose life was completely altered at the moment their name was written. So much humanity is inscribed on these stones. Stone represents permanence. We carve the names of loved ones on tombstones after they die so they won't be forgotten. We use names on other memorials, too, such as streets, buildings, bridges, and schools. If the name lives on, so will the memory or legacy of the person who carried that name.

When we want to remember someone who has passed, was lost, or has a legacy that should not be forgotten, we ensure that their spirit and what they represent to us live on by saying their name. Speaking their name, we feel their presence even after they are gone.

We've established that a name is the key to your identity, your power, and your individuality. Now forget all that. You are not your name.

Regardless of what you are called now, you have lived before, in different bodies with different names. You have been many people, all with unique identities. That doesn't mean the importance of your name is diminished in any way. All of those other names also represented an individual, a journey, and a life. These past-life personas experienced love, joy, pain, disappointment, and everything else that comes with being human.

I'm sure you have some questions.

You are probably wondering why I made such a case for how critical your name is, only to tell you that you aren't your name. It's true that a name contains identity, humanity, a life, and because you have all of the above, I want you to know that you also had that same depth of existence in all your past lives. I want you to begin to think of your past lives as less theoretical or ethereal, and more in terms of discovering a person who you were—and still are.

I want your past lives to become real people to you. Those people had names, certainly. But who were they? What did they desire? What did they accomplish? What made them proud? What were their failures or limitations? Whom did they love? What did they value?

It is true that your past-life personas lived, well, in the past, in other countries, as different genders, within other cultures. We will get into the specifics of all that in much greater detail later, but for now, just consider the individuals you have been before.

Give your past-life selves the power, the individuality, and the humanity of having been born to a family who gave them a name. That doesn't mean you should demand that your family and friends begin to call you by one of your former names. That life has come and gone; it is in the past. You are living again, in a new body, with a new lifetime here on Earth, and with a new name.

MEDITATION MOMENT

Find a comfortable spot to sit or lie down in a quiet place where you won't be disrupted.

Close your eyes and take a few deep breaths. Do your best to relax.

Now, imagine that you are in an enormous house made of many, many rooms.

As you walk through this house, you stop and visit each room. In each, you discover a different person.

These people represent your past-life selves. Allow your imagination to wander, to run free, without worrying about what is real or imagined.

Perhaps your past-life selves are doing everyday things, like cooking, relaxing, or sleeping.

As you watch yourself in previous lives, look around each room you enter and notice the details inside.

What decorations are on the walls?

What languages are used on the covers of books?

What clothes are the people wearing?

Do they seem healthy and happy, or do they seem to be struggling physically or emotionally?

As you visit the people in each room, speak to them in your mind. Ask them their name, and wait for them to answer.

When you are finished with this exercise, write down the details you observed and the names of the people—your incarnations—you met.

There. Now, some of your past lives have names.

Because you have had other names, that is why you are *not* your name. You have had many, many names. By thinking about your past lives as individuals who also had names, you give those people their dignity, individuality, power, and humanity. Perhaps by embracing your past selves in this way, you can better appreciate who you are right here and now.

Did it work? If not, no need to worry! Sometimes exercises like this take practice, and some days you are more relaxed and open to imagining your past selves than other days. You can try again if you couldn't see the rooms or the people inside. Keep in mind that some people just are not visual and don't use their mind's eye; they often use their inner knowing instead. So if you didn't see anything this time, try again and perhaps you'll "just know" who is in your rooms.

You can experience your own imagination in lots of ways.

TOOLS TO DEVELOP

LEARN YOUR *"CLAIR-"*S

We are all intuitive. Yes, some of us were born with a little bit more of a gift in this area, but anyone who is interested can learn and develop these skills.

In fact, we all have intuitive or psychic experiences all the time, even if our culture doesn't speak openly about how common it is. For example, a dream is a psychic experience, as is a gut feeling that you get about something. Many of us feel presences or what we call vibes or energy.

Uncovering your past-life memories is also an intuitive experience, one I believe is available to almost everyone—if you are willing to be patient and learn how to do it.

We all have unique ways of experiencing intuitive information. Some of us "see" things in our mind, while others feel or just know. Some people hear a voice speaking to them, smell something they can't track to a specific source, or get a taste in their mouth that alerts them to something that they need to notice or pay attention to.

We each have five senses, but we also have what I like to call our extra senses, which are used to pick up on intuitive information. All intuitive experiences involve extrasensory perception, or ESP, but there is not just one "sixth sense."

We are constantly discovering ways the human brain perceives information, so this list of extra senses is not exhaustive and will change as our understanding of intuition and how it works develops. The "clair-"s we do know about include:

Clairvoyance, or "inner sight"

Clairsentience, or "inner feeling"

Claircognizance, or "inner knowing"

Clairaudience, or "inner hearing"

Clairalience, or "inner smelling"

Clairgustance, or "inner tasting"

Take a few moments and think about each of these "clair-"s. Can you can recall experiencing each of them, in a dream or meditation, on a walk or a drive, or just at a random moment?

Have you ever seen something happen in a dream? (If so, that's clairvoyance.) Did someone once say something to you that felt so true it gave you goosebumps? (Clairsentience.) Or have you ever met someone whom you just knew was not to be trusted? (That's claircognizance.) Have you ever heard a voice that seemed to come from inside your own head? (Clairaudience.) Have you ever smelled a perfume, cigar smoke, or something cooking that you could not find the source of? (Clairalience.) Finally, did you ever walk into a room that had a bad vibe and then notice a weird, metallic taste in your mouth? (Clairgustance.)

Some of you will have noted only one or two of these, whereas others might have experienced all of them. Each of your own personal "*clair-*"s is how you experience intuitive information, which includes your past lives experienced in the meditations and exercises throughout this book.

So take note of yours, because that is a clue to your unique intuitive abilities and where you should focus when you want to tap into your inner knowledge or your own intuition.

two

YOU ARE NOT
YOUR LOOKS

When was the last time you looked into a mirror? Perhaps it was earlier today, checking out your reflection as a part of your morning routine. Most of us have several mirrors throughout our homes that we use on a regular basis; we also encounter them in public spaces, in our workplaces, in our cars, and even on our phones' cameras. In fact, mirrors are so commonplace that you probably look at your reflection so frequently you don't even think about it.

A mirror is a tool that allows you to view what others see when they look at you. It offers a reflection of your physical form, your body, the anatomical figurative design you have come to know as you—your face, features, hair, limbs, and overall shape.

In fact, despite having the knowledge that we have lived before, in many past lives, most of us have formed at least part of our sense of self around the way we look. Our looks are intricately connected with our identity and how we think of ourselves. When asked who we are, we may even answer by describing ourselves in terms of physical features.

You might tell people you are a tall woman with dark, curly hair. Or a man of average height with an athletic build who is slightly balding. Or the petite blond standing next to the dark-haired man with green eyes. You get the picture.

THOUGHT-PROVOKING

How would you describe yourself to someone who was looking to identify you in a crowd?

What features would you list?

What is unique about your appearance?

Perhaps by noticing our culture's preoccupation with mirrors, we can realize that this fixation is reflecting a much deeper truth, that an abiding fascination with physical looks is stitched into our society. With the advent of technology such as photography and videography, visual images have become hugely prominent and important in our world. The invention of social media combined with the phenomenon of a camera on every phone and the normalization of the art of the selfie have created what could be called an obsession with appearance.

But here's the thing: who you are has nothing to do with your body or your looks. When you lived before, you had totally different features because you had a body that had nothing to do with the life you are embodying right now. When one life ends, your body dies and ceases to exist. But *you* do not cease to exist. Who you actually are lives on in a new body. That means that your looks, or how you appear physically, is not your true identity. You might consider that your reflection shows who you are, but that is only who you appear to be right now.

Becoming aware of your past lives, with the varied physical features you have worn across many lifetimes, can help you see that identifying with your appearance is a false identity because it is only one aspect of the bigger picture.

GET CREATIVE

In celebration of the body you have right now, the one allowing you to have the life you are living today, I would like you to create a self-portrait.

It can be in any medium, whether a sketch, drawing, painting, or even a photo you take of yourself.

As you create this self-portrait, I want you to focus on your features and traits that you enjoy and feel the most confident about.

What do you look like in your mind's eye?

I don't want you to judge your portrait or overanalyze it; instead, notice how you portray yourself and how it makes you feel when you focus on the parts of your face or body that are the most beautiful and unique to you.

This obsession we have with our looks—and the belief that our looks make up our identity—is not a new concept. When exploring ancient art from cultures around the globe, it is interesting to note that figurative portraits designed to capture one's looks or likeness are almost as old as humanity itself, with seventeen-thousand-year-old cave drawings depicting animals and humans.

As artistic renderings evolved over time, they continued to portray both literal and symbolic figures, as many works of art included depictions of gods and goddesses or other religious figures in human form. For centuries, the act of being captured in clay or on canvas was often only available to a select, privileged few and designed to show their wealth and power.

One can easily imagine that the subjects of these works of art would gaze at their image and think, *Yes, that's me*. From then on, that rendering would serve as an enduring representation of both the person and their identity in the world. Wealthy, powerful families often still display portraits of their ancestors in their homes as a way of maintaining a connection with that deceased person's identity—and the origins of their prestige.

It is likely that through this process of creating art, different cultures began to establish standards of beauty or features that were considered desirable and attractive. Artists then chose to highlight those traits in their renderings of celestial figures such as Aphrodite, Lakshmi, the Virgin Mary and Jesus, King David, Buddha, and more.

When commissioned to paint a portrait of a king, queen, or other important person, the artists would make similar small alterations to portray their subject as more desirable, perhaps tweaking the shape and size of the nose, eyes, lips, ears, or other features to please their patron (the original Photoshop!). Each image held a robust sense of identity and political weight, so altering it bolstered the person's status to be more godlike, desirable, and powerful.

But because we associate our identity so closely with our appearance, this can and often does go wrong very quickly. If any of our features happens to lie outside what is accepted as beautiful in our culture or time period, we too often tend to view them as flaws or imperfections. Obviously, such standards change over time and are different depending on a variety of circumstances, but the fact remains that we have rules for what is considered attractive or not.

Beyond that, our appearance often becomes connected to our feelings of inherent worthiness as a person. There is an epidemic today, especially among young people, of depression, low self-esteem, and even self-harm or suicide due to these complicated feelings around body image. In our capitalist culture of constant self-improvement, it isn't easy to avoid the trap of trying to fit a certain ideal. In fact, we often go out of our way to alter our appearance in an attempt to better fit those imposed standards, whether via diets, laser treatments, exercise fads, pills and tonics, or plastic surgery.

Many of us also struggle with aging because our society also pushes the idea that beauty is the counterpart of youth. More and more people are waking up to the fact that with age comes wisdom and people in every phase of life have a critical role to play in a functioning society. But there is still so much work to do to move away from the fallacy that someone with the "wrong" body holds less value. Too many of us still think we *are* our body.

I once worked with a woman who was struggling with getting older and how her body was changing, particularly after a traumatic divorce that was triggered by her husband's affair with a much younger woman. After more than twenty-five years of marriage, she suddenly found herself single in her mid-fifties and was overwhelmed just thinking about putting herself out there and dating again.

Under my consult, she had a vivid past-life experience as a woman in a tribal culture who had lived to be well into her nineties. She described how frail her body felt, how thin her skin had become, and how her hair was completely white and her face was covered with wrinkles. But she had been considered a wise woman in her tribe, and she got emotional when she described how revered and respected she had been.

She now understood that her age had given her earned wisdom, that she was beautiful, and that her body had a certain grace after serving her with health and strength for so many years. After this powerful past-life experience, she decided to embrace her natural beauty and step into her inner sage as an older woman with much wisdom to share.

Not long after this, she met a man who was drawn to her power and confidence. She remarried and is now enjoying her golden years with the love of her life.

Now, it is certainly true that we do have agency with how we present ourselves and the choices we can make that will alter our appearance, based on personal preference. We can choose what we wear, what our own personal style is, and what fashion statements represent our inner self or personality. We can choose how we style our hair, whether we color it a different shade and make

DREAMWORK

Before you go to bed tonight, I would like you to spend a few minutes sitting quietly and setting an intention to have a meaningful dream that allows you to see and experience what it is like to be in a different body than the one you have right now.

It doesn't matter if you ask your spirit guides to grant you this dream or simply consult your own unconscious mind, but ask whatever source feels right for you.

This dream can be a past-life dream, where you experience being in a body you had before. It can be fantasy, from a movie, book, or play. Or you can choose to have a dream from the perspective of someone you know.

Keep in mind that this might not work right away, so be patient and try again another night if it doesn't work for you the first time.

When you wake up, be sure to record your thoughts and feelings about how it felt to be in a different body in your dream.

our curly hair straight or our straight hair curly. We can use our looks and appearance as a tool to let our inner light shine and represent how we want the world to see us.

Certain more permanent body alterations allow us to express ourselves, our beliefs, our background, or our culture. Many people get tattoos or piercings, which are outward expressions of the way you choose to identify or show your ties to a specific group. My great-uncle had a tattoo of a bulldog on his forearm, which he got during World War II to show his loyalty to the Marine Corps.

Many cultures practice tattooing or piercing to celebrate rites of passage and accomplishments or as a way to identify themselves as a part of a tribe or a people, including the Maori people of New Zealand, Indian brides (who use henna), and, historically, certain indigenous American peoples (although this tradition was later suppressed by missionaries). Among some ethnic groups in Africa, tattoos are seen as a way to provide a person with spiritual protection; heal an illness; show an affili-

DIG DEEPER

What are some of the choices you make about how you present yourself?

Consider how you dress, how you style your hair, any tattoos or piercings you have, etc. What message about your personality or lifestyle do these convey?

Now think back to an earlier period in your life and consider how your choices about your appearance have changed since then.

Has your style shifted or evolved?

What inner changes to your sense of identity did these changes reflect?

Are the person you are today and the person you were at that earlier point in your life the same?

How have the alterations you made to your appearance and how you present yourself physically reflected those inner shifts?

ation with a particular tribe; and reflect attributes that a person might possess, such as courage, wisdom, and social status.

Many people struggle to accept their body, but the irony is that the body you have right now, the one you were born with, was the body you *chose* in this life. Yes, you chose all of the circumstances of your birth before you reincarnated, including the way you would look. I believe that you chose the body, including all of your features as well as gender and gender expression, that would best help you fulfill your purpose and give you the best opportunity for learning and growth.

Some people are blessed with beauty, or at least what society has decided is beautiful, and others might not be. Both come with their challenges. But when you realize that you have had many different bodies that have looked many different ways, you can see that the beauty in all of us is much deeper than our skin, hair, eyes, and features.

Our beauty is inherent; it is inner. When it becomes clear that who you are is not your body, the beauty within shines through, and you recognize that beauty in others as well.

So many of us fall victim to overidentifying with our looks, or even obsessing over them, which can create a false identity that prevents us from being connected to the part of us that is not our body. I'm talking about your soul. Your soul is that inner light that survives death and reincarnates into a new body many times across many lifetimes. It is the eternal and wise inner you.

Your soul is the real you. Not your body.

The term for "soul" in ancient Greek is *psyche*, which is the root of the words *psychology* and *psychoanalysis*. It can also be

A LITTLE DIRECTION

IT DOESN'T MATTER WHAT YOU CALL IT

Many people use the term *soul* or *spirit* to describe who we are on the inside, or the piece of ourselves that reincarnates and lives many lives. But you could also call it your inner self; your higher self; your authentic self; your true self; or your consciousness, essence, nature, or being.

Some people prefer to stay away from terms that seem either religious or too New Age, so feel free to use whatever word feels right for you. It doesn't matter what you call it; all describe the same thing.

translated as "spirit," "mind," "life," or "breath" and is where we get the words *psyched*, *psycho*, *psychedelic*, *psychotic*, and *psychological*, all of which describe states of the mind.

We also get the term *psychic* from this root, which comes from the Greek word *psychikos*, or "of the soul." The Greeks, as well as the majority of ancient cultures, held a belief that the mind and the soul were the same and that any healing of the mind also required a healing of the soul, or spirit.

After generations of separating the mind from the body in the Western medical paradigm, we've come full circle. Many practitioners today allow for an integrated approach, with the understanding that the healing of the mind can also be a spiritual process, instead of just treating disorders with drugs designed to alter the brain and physical body. In fact, many doctors and scientists have opened themselves to the idea that they are treating not just a body, but a mind and a soul as well.

Now, even though you are not your body, because you have had many other bodies in your many other lives, that doesn't mean you don't need your body. It is absolutely true that your body is a temple because it is currently housing your beautiful, eternal soul. Your body is a vessel to carry out the work you have reincarnated on planet Earth to do, and caring for it is not only necessary but vital.

The analogy I like to make is that your body is the car and you (aka your soul) are the driver. As the driver, you regularly have to change the oil, check the brakes, air up the tires, and be sure there is enough gas in the tank to get you where you want to go. It is important to focus on your health and wellness, eat nourishing foods, exercise, get enough sleep, and see your doctor to support and sustain your vessel.

Not all of us were born with healthy, vibrant bodies. And even if we were born with a strong body and blessed with good health, sometimes, by no fault of our own, our bodies don't stay that way. People have disabilities, chronic pain, disease, autoimmune issues, and much more. Some of us are sick or unwell for many years. Many of us do and will die from disease, and not everyone gets to fully enjoy life as a healthy person.

But you did choose the body you were born with in this life, and your decision was based on how you could best learn, grow, and fulfill your purpose for reincarnating and being here right now. Sometimes we chose bodies that are not as healthy and strong in order to have that experience, to challenge ourselves.

Sometimes that challenge is also for your loved ones and the people around you because caregiving is a meaningful lesson and experience as well.

Yes, you are a soul, but you are inhabiting a body, and although discovering and connecting with your soul is a necessary process, it is also essential that you find ways to be present within your body. That's easier said than done. It is often difficult to be fully present in your body, as is evident by the various forms of escapism that many of us engage in. Some people use drugs or alcohol to avoid having to be in their bodies, or they spend a lot of time watching screens, becoming workaholics, or overexercising.

MEDITATION MOMENT

BE IN YOUR BODY

Take a moment and find a comfortable place to sit, preferably with your feet on the floor or ground in front of you.

Close your eyes, and take several very deep breaths.

Inhale deeply, and exhale completely.

And as you breathe, I want you to turn your attention to your body.

How do you feel? Are you tired? Tense? Relaxed?

Do you notice any tightness or pain anywhere?

I want you to imagine yourself sending some of your deep breaths to any spot or area of your body that you feel might need them.

Now I want you to place your hands on top of your thighs, lightly resting them in your lap.

Feel your thighs, and notice any sensation you might experience as you connect with them.

Now focus on your sit bones, your pelvis, and the chair or surface you are sitting or resting on.

Really notice how you are sitting, and feel the surface connect with your body.

Now I want you to shift your attention to both of your feet, which are now firmly and evenly planted on the ground.

Feel the floor or ground beneath you, and feel your feet join with the surface they are resting on.

I want you to sit with your feet on the ground, and with your hands on your thighs, feeling your seat in the chair or other surface for a few minutes while you continue to take deep breaths.

Connect deeply with your body, and feel how present you are inside of it.

And send some gratitude to this incredible vessel, your physical form that your soul is currently occupying.

When you can accept that you are not your looks, or even your body, you can build a new identity for yourself that includes your past lives, when you had different features and shapes and sizes. Love your body. Worship it. But understand that how you look is not you.

MEDITATION MOMENT

MIRRORS AND FACES

For this exercise, you need a mirror. It can be a handheld mirror or one that's hanging on the wall; the size doesn't matter.

If you can, dim the lights. I don't want you in complete darkness, but rather in very low light. Perhaps you can close the blinds or curtains and light a candle.

Sit with your mirror in this low light in a place that is comfortable.

Take a few deep breaths, relaxing your body and quieting your mind.

Gaze into your mirror and look at your reflection.

Continue to breathe deeply, and as you do, soften your gaze.

Allow your face and the rest of the image reflected in the mirror to begin to blur and become less sharp.

Keep taking deep breaths.

Now, as you softly gaze at your reflection, ask yourself, out loud or to yourself:

Who am I?

Am I really me?

I want you to really dig into this line of self-inquiry.

Notice how these questions make you feel.

As you continue to breathe and repeat these questions, keeping your gaze soft in the mirror, notice what you see or how your image changes.

Many people observe their features shifting, and many even see what looks like different faces or images come into awareness as they softly gaze into the mirror.

These shifting images may represent your various past lives, the faces you have had before in previous incarnations.

Some people even notice features of animals, such as mammals or birds, emerge.

Take notice of all of the different faces that arise when you ask yourself these questions.

Then, close your eyes for a moment, take a deep breath, and say either out loud or to yourself:

I am in this body right now.

Open your eyes, and gaze upon your current face.

Send yourself gratitude and love for choosing this form, this face, and this body for your current life.

three

YOU ARE NOT
YOUR RACE OR ETHNICITY

Human beings come in many different colors and shades. Some of us are light-skinned, some are dark-skinned, and others are every variation in between. Skin color is often a distinguishing factor in how we recognize someone's ethnicity or race, which is connected to what part of the world or continent their ancestors originated from.

These variations in skin color or pigmentation are due to evolution and the human body's incredible ability to adapt. Because every country on every continent has a different climate and conditions specific to that environment, over time, as humans were born and lived in various places, their bodies developed physical traits that allowed them not only to survive but to thrive.

For example, in warmer climates, the skin produces more melanin, a substance in the body responsible for skin, hair, and eye color. Melanin is produced in larger amounts in sunnier climates because it is the body's natural defense against the damaging rays of the sun. The amount of melanin each individual produces is based on their genetic blueprint and how much sun exposure their ancient ancestors had. So in areas close to the equator and, therefore, warmer and sunnier, people have darker skin, hair, and eyes than people who live in colder, darker climates. Someone who has ancestry from Somalia, which sits right on the equator, likely has much darker skin than someone who is a descendant of a person who hailed from Finland, a country that is much farther north and has a much colder climate.

But even though we understand the science, skin color and race too often motivate misunderstanding, bias, discrimination, prejudice, bigotry, injustice, violence, subjugation, bondage, captivity, slavery, and genocide.

But guess what? We have all lived before, in many past lives. Your past lives are diverse, both ethnically and racially. This is because you haven't lived in just one location over and over again; you have lived on every continent and many countries in order to have a variety of experiences as a human being. We all have had different cultural backgrounds, rituals that created meaning in our lives, clothing that we wore, and foods that we enjoyed. At night, we all looked up and saw the stars in the sky from various vantage points, but the stars were all the same.

If you only ever reincarnated in one place, into one group or tribe or ethnicity, that would completely defeat the purpose of reincarnation, which is to learn and grow. And if you are given the same lesson again and again, in the same country and wearing the same skin, then you are not maximizing your potential for gaining new insight, perspective, and wisdom.

Even so, many of us strongly identify with our race or ethnicity. In so many ways, this is a good thing, to honor our ancestors and the storied lineage of the family members who have come before us. To be proud of your ancestry, your people, and all that they overcame to create your family and open the door to your life today is a key element in knowing who you are through the lens of race or ethnicity. In fact, many cultures, particularly those that are a part of ethnic minorities, hold extra tight to their identity because their survival has depended on it.

But let's broaden the lens. Yes, you are who you are today in part because you were born into a family with its own ancestry, but you have lived in many other families with many different backgrounds. Just like your appearance, your race or ethnicity does not make up the entire picture.

THOUGHT-PROVOKING

How do you identify?

What race, ethnicity, background, or culture do you connect to?

How did you come to form that identity?

We tend to use certain umbrella categories when defining race, such as Black or white, but within these larger groups is a tremendous amount of diversity. For example, here in the United

States, on the government census, the only choices offered are Black or African American, white or European, Hispanic, American Indian or Alaska Native, Asian, or Native Hawaiian or other Pacific Islander.

What if you have one parent who is from one category and one from another? Or what if, over hundreds of years, your ancestors intermixed and intermarried by way of migration and immigration?

In fact, most of us are mixed race, and the presence and popularity of DNA tests has shown that this blending of ethnic backgrounds has been prevalent. Of course, at least some of this mixing of ethnicities reflects a dark past that includes rape, violence, and the subjugation of peoples or groups to establish supremacy and power. Many of us have a hard time acknowledging the tragic side of our DNA history, for the descendants of the oppressors as well as the oppressed. But we must confront this truth to find a path to reconciliation, to a collective healing of intergenerational trauma, and to stopping racist attitudes and actions.

The science of DNA research is doing a lot to move us forward in the direction of understanding that we are all humans with varied expressions of our unique gene sequences. By exploring the ways that we share our humanity, rather than by focusing on our differences, we can forge a path toward love, peace, equality, and understanding. Uncovering your own varied and diverse past lives can be a powerful way to see that underneath our skin, we are all the same and a part of one single human race.

This biological mixing and blending is integral to our mod-

JOURNAL TIME

WHAT DO YOU KNOW ABOUT YOUR ANCESTRY?

Take a moment and write down everything you know about your ancestry.

Have you or anyone in your family taken a DNA test?

If so, what did you discover about your family roots?

What are some of the stories you have been told about where your people come from?

Did your parents' marriage represent a blending of cultures?

How do you identify racially, ethnically, and culturally?

ern world, too, with technology allowing for unprecedented levels of migration and immigration, exploration and exposure to other cultures. Many places have developed a unique cultural identity over time to integrate aspects of the people indigenous to the area and immigrants or other foreigners who have settled there. For example, southern Spain's proximity to North Africa ushered in a combination of food, music, art, architecture, language, and learning—including science and philosophy—that is unlike the rest of the Iberian Peninsula. Meanwhile, northern Spain has Celtic roots, which may surprise tourists who are expecting to find flamenco and tapas but instead discover bagpipes, stone circles, and pagan solstice rituals there (along with a handful of other languages).

DIG DEEPER

I want you to take a few moments and think about your cultural or ethnic identity and how you express it.

How have your family background and identity followed you through your life?

Have you blended the culture or cultures of your heritage with a new culture, based on a place where you live or one you have been exposed to?

How is your own, unique cultural blend reflected in your life?

Emigration away from the place of one's ancestry or birth has happened throughout history, whether due to war, famine, religious or cultural oppression, or capture and enslavement. (Women in particular were often expected to leave their family homes for their husband's.) Others left their ancestral homes to seek opportunities, jobs, or wealth. Stories of conquerors who pillaged and ravaged to take power are often glamorized because history is most often written or told by the winner. The fact that human beings have never stayed in one place is what gave us the concept of the "other," as well as the idea of a certain population within a larger one as a minority group that may be conquered, enslaved, systematically marginalized, and oppressed.

Today, we are having conversations about correcting this history to reflect the truth as witnessed and experienced by all people, not just the victors. The truth is not always pretty, but it is vital that it is told from every side for society to move forward in a new, better way. Understanding the past is the key to creating the future, and this is true about both our past lives and our collective history.

When you understand that you have lived many lives as various ethnicities, as numerous races, and with different skin colors, the idea of the "other" becomes obsolete. Any identity based on tribalism—and the associated attitudes and behavior—is a false one. Your life now is just one small piece of your entire ancestral story. It is human nature to feel connected to people who look like you, but excavating your past lives can help you open the curtain wider to discover that although we all look different, inside we are all the same.

Whenever my clients experience their past lives as different ethnicities and races, it is a profound moment for them. The experience of seeing themselves in an unfamiliar body, sometimes with the recognition that they are speaking another language than their current one, can jolt them out of the idea that they can identify in any way with the color of their skin.

I once worked with a client from Haiti who was a dark-skinned Black woman. She had a vivid past-life memory as a white woman with fair skin and light hair and eyes. She found this hilarious and was laughing during the past-life experience, saying she couldn't believe she had been white. Her past life represented such a distinctly different experience and identity that she found humor in it.

I have also had clients who identify as white find out that they were Black, Hispanic, Native American, or Asian in a past life. Even though you might identify as a certain race or ethnicity, know that your identity is mutable. It holds nuance. Getting to know your diverse past lives increases your understanding and empathy both for yourself and for others.

A LITTLE DIRECTION

IS IT APPROPRIATION OR APPRECIATION?

We have lived as many skin colors, races, and ethnicities. This variety of experiences across many lifetimes teaches us compassion, empathy, and appreciation for different cultures and backgrounds.

But just because you had a life in which you were a different race or from another culture, particularly if that group is a minority of any kind, does not mean you understand what it means to have chosen that life or path—or can claim that identity today. You have chosen a different form in this lifetime, so although you can appreciate a culture, be sure you are not appropriating one.

Learning about your diverse past lives is not cultural appropriation. It is simply a fact. We have all been Black, white, brown, and more. Cultural appropriation would be if we used that fact to lay claim on that background in *this* life. You can't know what it is like to be a different race, group, ethnicity, or people, but you can enhance your understanding of what that experience means.

These diverse past-life experiences are why we feel more drawn to certain cultures and places than others. Having lived a past life in a place that is foreign to us today can create an abiding fascination. This can show up in music that moves you, movies that you watch again and again because they celebrate a specific country, ethnic foods that you love, or works of art that speak to you because they feature a certain background or racial identity.

Some people have discovered that they had unconsciously known a previous identity by considering their favorite places to travel to or the cultures that elicit feelings of peace, belonging, or longing. I have heard many people say that they traveled to a new country or continent and "just knew" their way around or felt that culturally specific smells or sounds triggered emotions in them.

I once worked with a woman, a white American of European descent, who said that the first time she traveled to Istanbul she instinctively knew where the streets she had been wandering led to. The smells of food and spices in the air were familiar, as if she had been there before. She described this experience as a "lost memory," like it was something she knew she should remember but wouldn't quite take form in her mind's eye.

She told me that hearing the call for prayer from one of the many beautiful mosques in the city caused her to burst into tears. A lot of emotions surfaced on that trip but primarily a sadness and a longing for what felt like another time that existed both in a faraway place and just under the surface of her memory and consciousness.

Neither of us were surprised when she recalled a past life as a Muslim woman in Istanbul in the seventeenth century. The memory simply confirmed what she already knew to be true: she had lived in that place before.

I hear all kinds of stories about this phenomenon of being

DREAMWORK

OTHER TIMES AND OTHER PLACES

I want you to take a few minutes tonight before you go to bed to set an intention to have a dream that features one of your past lives in a place that is foreign to you.

You can set this intention by thinking about it, saying it out loud, or—even more powerful—journaling your intention and then keeping your journal beside your bed while you sleep.

Include in your intention that you experience multiple aspects of the culture connected to this past life in your dream, including the color or shade of your skin, manner of dress and clothing, food, and music.

Ask your spirit guides to show you a dream that is vivid and colorful, and one with which you can feel a powerful emotional attachment.

When you wake, be sure to write down immediately what came to you, before the details of the dream begin to fade.

drawn to specific cultures across time. I once worked with a man who was obsessed with Japanese samurai culture and knew everything about it, despite being an African American man in this life.

When I was a child, I was fascinated with Native American culture, particularly the tribes in the American West such as the Lakota and Arapahoe. I maintain a deep, abiding respect for this culture. I am dedicated to causes connected to indigenous rights and have studied Native American spiritual and healing traditions for many years. Even though I do believe I was Native

American in a past life, this doesn't mean I get to claim a Native identity for my own. Rather, my affinity with a community outside my own fosters curiosity, insight, and an understanding that I never would have achieved if I remained rigidly tied to a narrow sense of identity.

Over time, as you discover that you have been Black and brown and white and have lived on every continent, you can also find the key to our shared humanity that has nothing to do with race (while also never forgetting that the consequences and lived experiences of being one race or another in our white-supremacist society are very real). Reincarnation teaches us that these perceived differences are surface-level only and have nothing to do with who we are on a spiritual level.

JOURNAL TIME

Take a few moments to think about some of the places and cultures that you are drawn to but that are not your own.

Is there a country you have always wanted to visit or a place you have traveled to where you just felt at home?

Are there any cultures or time periods about which you enjoy watching films or reading books?

Are you drawn to artwork, jewelry, or clothing in the style of a different culture?

These represent your positive cultural associations. Now, go through the same exercise, but instead of focusing on the cultures you feel positively toward, think about ones you do *not* like or feel drawn to.

Are there any cultures that you find to be scary or heavy in some way—unpleasant or dirty, perhaps?

Please don't judge yourself; most people can identify strong feelings of attraction and repulsion in this scenario. Just notice what comes up and write it down.

Now you have two categories in your notebook: people and places you love, and people and places you would rather not connect with.

It has been my experience that anytime you have a strong reaction to a place or people, good or bad, that is an indicator that you may have had a past-life experience as a member of that group.

For now, just take note of what comes up for you in both categories.

four

YOU ARE NOT
YOUR GENDER OR SEXUALITY

Are you a man or a woman? For many, this might seem like a simple question with only two answers, based on the sex you were assigned at birth.

But we are beginning to understand more and more that this is a nuanced query with many possible answers. This cultural shift about what constitutes gender suggests that it's so much deeper than our physical sex characteristics. Gender is more of a range or spectrum based on how each of us identifies. The male-female binary has expanded to include identities such as gender-neutral, gender-fluid, gender-expansive, transgender, nonbinary, and more.

This is an amazing development for the many people whose identity lies beyond cisgender (when your sex assigned at birth and the gender with which you identify align). This increased freedom means there have also been changes in what is considered acceptable in terms of gender expression—or "boy" versus "girl" behavior and appearance.

The last few decades have also brought significant shifts in traditional gender roles both in the home and in the workplace. In your past lives, even the more recent ones, you likely had to endure many more rules about gender expectations and norms than you do now.

But in many cultures, gender identity expectations still begin at birth, as hospitals label each new human "boy" or "girl," depending on their sex traits, and put them in blue or pink clothes

REVISIONIST HISTORY

There are many trends today toward gender-neutral clothing and toys because it has been discovered that toys "for boys" were more educational and career-centered and toys "for girls" focused more on developing a role as a caregiver or nurturer in the home.

Giving children gender-neutral toys frees their imagination about their future potential and has allowed children of all genders to explore careers and interests that are not defined by traditional expectations.

What toys and objects were you drawn to as a child? How did you play?

Were you expected to adhere to certain gender-specific toys or hobbies?

How can you connect that to who you have become and how you identify today?

accordingly. (This trend of dressing babies in gender-specific clothing only became popular in the 1940s. Before that, most people dressed babies in frilly white dresses—for easy diaper access—regardless of sex.)

This idea of clothing as being gender related is ancient and present in every culture on Earth, but so is the history of those who have defied the rules and dressed differently than the gender they were assigned at birth. Not only that, but what we think of as "male" versus "female" clothing also has shifted over time (see Louis XIV wearing high heels or Shakespearean theater troupes in drag). Many societies still insist on outward gender conformity, but many other places have loosened up around how you choose to identify and express gender in your clothes, hair, makeup, body language, and voice.

And of course, you might be a man right now, but you likely have been a woman in a past life, and vice versa. In fact, over the years, I have learned that when I dive into a specific incarnation with my clients, about 50 percent of the time, they have chosen a different gender. Among all the qualities and characteristics that vary from life to life, many folks identify most strongly with their gender, so this revelation can be a particularly stunning one.

The shocking realization that who I thought I was, based on my gender, was a false identity set in suddenly the first time I experienced a past life. In my mind's eye, I looked down and saw that I had large, rough, masculine hands and a male body. I do identify strongly with being a feminine, cisgender woman in this life, but there I was as a man. It immediately changed the way I looked at myself.

I once had a client, a cisgender man, who had a powerful

GET CREATIVE

YOURSELF AS ANOTHER GENDER

I want you to create a likeness of yourself, but one that is another gender than what you identify with now.

This likeness can be a drawing, sketch, or painting, or it can be a photograph or video you make of yourself as a different gender expression.

What are the features of this new gender expression?

What clothing do you wear? How do you style your hair?

What is your body language like? What about your posture and how you present?

What is different, or what has changed, by way of shifting your gender identity?

Have fun with this!

past-life experience as a woman. This took place in a tribal setting in Africa, and his past-life self was not wearing much clothing. He could see his naked breasts and body, which was an experience that left him in awe of the female form and the fact that he had lived before as a woman. He recalled being tenacious and resourceful, balancing his duties as a mother to several small children with household duties and chores that included walking for several miles a day to gather fresh water and prepare meals that fed many people. After this experience, he saw his wife and female employees with a new perspective, as he realized that women still manage to balance these same duties and often have to work much harder than men because they work both in and out of the home.

That brings me to my next point: the occurrence of living as one gender or another always has been divergent. Being born a boy across space and time is a distinct experience from being born a girl, and each has its own challenges and lessons. This is still true. I don't have to tell you that the female or feminine experience often comes with oppression, less freedom, fewer opportunities, and violence. Sexism is nearly as old as time itself.

Much of this inequity has been blamed on biology; men are often considered to be stronger and have more stamina, and women are equipped to give birth and be caregivers. These stereotypes have long been used to perpetuate the patriarchy. Women have been dismissed, belittled, and diminished. They have been denied rights such as getting an education, voting, holding jobs outside the home, opening bank accounts, making their own reproductive choices, and having the same freedoms men have to decide aspects of their own lives and bodies such as where they are allowed to go and how they should dress. Women have been sexually exploited, raped, groped, and forced into submission. They have been feared and misunderstood, judged by their looks, stoned to death for imagined crimes, and burned as witches.

I have worked with quite a few women who have past lives that feature this kind of oppression and violence, and many were carrying unconscious fears about speaking their truth or stepping into their power from those memories. Uncovering these fears gave the women a chance to reclaim their agency because they were able to see that even though they had endured these crimes long ago, they had a chance to live a new narrative today.

It is true that there are many more opportunities for women and girls today, but unfortunately, misogyny and prejudice against women is not just historical; it is still happening in nearly every country in the world. As with racial equality, we still have a lot of work to do to create a universal society that features true egalitarianism for men and women, as well as for people who choose to identify as any, or no, gender.

Because we have lived as both men and women, exploring those past-life memories can help us understand more about the experience of the other. After all, we are here on Earth to learn and grow. Because life as a man is often much different than life as a woman, no matter the time period, how would it make sense that we would receive only half of the lessons available to us, if we were only one gender? We have to be male and female and all other genders and expressions. Each of us has been male and female, masculine and feminine, cisgender, bigender, agender, and everything in between.

One of the most interesting things I have witnessed while working with my clients is when they take on the energy of one of their past-life selves after remembering being this other person. I have seen people channel their inner warrior, goddess, protector, or mother and use that masculine or feminine energy to live more fully today.

I once worked with a woman who was seeking a promotion to become partner in a prestigious law firm and competing with several men for the position. Although she was equally qualified, she was worried that she would lose this opportunity in favor of one of the men because the firm was predominantly male.

As we worked together, she recalled being a statesman or leader in what seemed like ancient Rome. She experienced herself as a powerful, confident man who led with courage and conviction, which allowed her to see herself as this persona and bring that statesman's energy to the table. Needless to say, she got the partnership. That capable individual was still inside her, and she was able to project that persona and achieve her goals.

A LITTLE DIRECTION

KNOW YOUR PRONOUNS

A lot of nuances are involved when we talk about gender.

One of the most amazing things happening today is that there is more freedom and acceptance around the idea that gender is a fluid concept and what most societies in history saw as a fixed issue is actually more of a spectrum. There is agency involved with the gender we choose to identify with—or not!

So it is perfectly acceptable, and even preferable, to ask someone to share with you what their pronouns are if they wish to, such as she/her, he/him, or they/them.

When you know someone's pronouns, you can address them respectfully based on how they choose to identify.

Exploring your past lives can help you see that you have not always identified with the gender you do now and that there were times when you expressed your gender in different ways.

Past-life work can be a powerful way to understand that the gender binary is not the only option and that although this concept might feel black-and-white to some of us, for others, it contains nuances and complexities.

When we understand that we have shifted our gender identity and the way we express it across many lifetimes, we can stop being so attached to that identity as who we are.

Even though it might feel modish in our society, the concept of gender fluidity and nonbinary identity is an ancient one. Instances of gender nonconforming figures have appeared in nearly every recorded society throughout history. Joan of Arc in fifteenth-century France and Hatshepsut, the female pharaoh who ruled ancient Egypt in 1400s BCE, both wore men's clothing and were depicted as androgynous. The Chevalier d'Éon, who was a cross-dressing, gender-bending spy in eighteenth-century France, was assigned male at birth but often dressed as a woman and even chose to live the second half of their life as a woman, with the king's blessing. These are just a handful of examples.

Many cultures, including ancient Greece, had virgins or eunuchs who served in holy temples, establishing a special kind of spirituality outside traditional gender roles or identity. In ancient Mesopotamia, there was a gender-ambiguous deity called Ishtar, and the priests of the cult of Ishtar presented as gender-neutral. In India, this third gender is called *hirja*, and these people are said to possess sacred powers that are contingent upon their asexuality. In Polynesia, this third gender, called *māhū*, is considered neither male or female, and they are the keepers of oral traditions, including the sacred hula dance. The māhū are still an integral part of the LGTBQIA+ community in Hawaii.

In many indigenous traditions, anyone who identified as a third "nongender" was often central in the community as spiritual leaders or keepers of wisdom. Today, some indigenous American cultures call people who are either transgender or gender nonconforming "Two Spirit," referring to the idea that these people carry within them the essence of both genders, with extra wisdom and insight befitting a sacred ceremonial role. (This concept itself is old, but the term *Two Spirit* only emerged in the twentieth century to describe anyone who holds a third-gender or gender-nonconforming position within the tribe. The original Navajo term translates to "one who changes," which emphasizes the fluidity of the identity.)

Needless to say, even with progress in our understanding and acceptance of nonbinary gender identity, many people still experience bias, prejudice, hate, and violence connected to their gender expression, including in the United States. It is yet another characteristic that is used as an opportunity to create a sense of otherness and division. That's why shifting how we look at gender through the lens of our own past lives can not only create empathy and understanding but also unite us in our universal commonalities.

Sexuality, or who you are attracted to, often gets grouped in with gender, but it is a separate (if related) issue. A lot of clients ask if the reason that someone might be gay or physically attracted to the opposite sex is because they had a past life as a different gender. I have not found this to be true. Our choice of gender in each life doesn't always impact who we are sexually attracted to, have romantic feelings toward, or choose to partner with.

DIG DEEPER

YIN AND YANG

In Eastern philosophy, there is a concept called yin and yang, as portrayed by this symbol. The idea is that duality creates balance.

In Chinese medicine, yin is considered feminine and yang is masculine.

The principle of yin and yang is that pairs of equal opposites attract and complement each other. They also are two parts of a whole and interdependent, meaning that one cannot exist without the other.

It also represents all dualities, including male and female, heaven and earth, dark and light, and the sun and the moon.

This beautiful concept and symbol recognizes that in order to achieve harmony, we need to interact with our opposites and counterparts.

Ultimately, the goal is to create balance and harmony within ourselves.

Because we all have lived many lives as male and female, and because we have had a variety of gender expressions, we all carry this duality within us. The goal is to become balanced beings, able to express equally our masculine and our feminine sides. Over our many lifetimes, we are learning to master the energy of both.

As with gender, we now have a better understanding of the complexities of human sexuality, and there are more rights available to people who are a part of the LGTBQIA+ community than ever before. But as with gender nonconformity, there is a long and arduous history of prejudice, hate, and violence against people who identify as gay, queer, etc.

I once worked with a woman who recalled being a man in what seemed like Asia, possibly China, in the early 1800s. When I asked her if she lived alone, she responded sadly that she did, but that she was deeply in love with someone she was forbidden to be with. Her beloved was another man with whom she worked—a man who was in love with her, too. She said there was a tremendous amount of heartbreak connected to this love. She remembered dying alone, sad and still longing for this man, this powerful soulmate.

She was able to find a healing around this sorrow, however, when she realized that this man whom she had loved so intensely had been reincarnated as the man who is her husband today. She was able to experience firsthand the truth that love is love, regardless of gender or sexuality. This experience renewed and strengthened her bond with her husband, as well as the level of appreciation they had for each other and the life they were privileged to share.

One of the most profound truths I have learned by watching my clients experience their past lives is that our soul, or who we are inside, has no gender. We reincarnate across many lifetimes as male, female, gay, straight, and everything in between. Having the variety of experiences that are unique to every gender identity, gender expression, and sexuality helps us learn, grow, and evolve.

Yes, you were assigned a sex at birth in this lifetime. You have a gender identity that is a part of the body that you chose and a sexual orientation in this life as well, but your soul has had a vast, cumulative experience as all of the possibilities of human form.

JOURNAL TIME

You are going to create a past-life persona who is a different gender than you are today.

Imagine yourself as either a man or a woman or another gender (i.e., who you imagine you were in a past life).

This past-life persona is the same age you are now. Give your past-life self a name.

What do you look like? Write down your physical appearance.

Are you short or tall?

What color is your hair?

What kind of clothes do you wear?

Describe the setting of this past-life experience.

What year or time period is it?

And where in the world do you live?

Don't judge what comes to mind; simply go with the first thing that comes to you.

Write down what you do with your time.

Do you work or have a career?

What fills your days?

What gives you joy and pleasure?

What are your challenges?

Give yourself a partner of any gender.

What do they look like?

What's their name?

Focus on how you feel about your partner, who can be real and based on a partner you have now or have imagined.

What thoughts do you have about your gender and the roles or expectations that come along with it?

What lessons did you learn from being that man, woman, or other that you can apply to your life today?

SECTION II

Live Your Present

five

YOU ARE NOT YOUR THOUGHTS OR BELIEFS

What are you thinking about right now?

Take a moment and notice what was on your mind before you started reading this chapter. I imagine that most of you had at least one thought come to mind, and many will have realized that multiple thoughts were kind of sitting there in your brain, waiting for attention to be drawn to them.

These thoughts may have included things on your to-do list, a worrisome interaction from earlier in the day, the realization that you are hungry or have a headache, or the anticipation that you will have to deal with something later. Our thoughts come and go all day long, even to the point that they may rob us of sleep.

They just keep coming.

Most of our thoughts have to do with either the past or the

future—reminiscing about or mulling over something that already happened, or worrying about something that hasn't happened yet.

Do any of these sound familiar?

I wish I hadn't said that.

I should have studied more for that test.

What am I going to make for dinner tonight?

This type of rumination is normal and likely an accurate depiction of our headspace on any given day.

At other times, our thoughts aren't about the past or future but instead have to do with something that is happening in the present moment:

I wonder why that person is being so rude.

My feet hurt when I walk.

Why is the sky blue?

Can you recall a time when you had absolutely no thoughts whatsoever? Maybe it was just a fleeting moment, but consider if you have ever had the experience of your mind being completely still. Most of us will find this much harder to reference because it isn't easy to do when our minds are constantly active. Controlling our thoughts and not allowing them to rule our emotions (and by extension our lives) is a practice we can approach in different ways.

One side effect of our thoughts, particularly when they're focused on the past or the future, is anxiety, the emotional reaction to dwelling on something we can't change or worrying about something in the future. I catch myself doing this all the time. I will be in the car, driving my kids to school, thinking about the coffee I spilled on the blouse I didn't have time to change out of, worrying about making it to my meeting on time. When I catch myself not being in the present moment, I try to take a deep breath and relax. Some days this is easier said than done. But learning to manage our thoughts is key to nourishing a healthy emotional center.

This idea of controlling your thoughts instead of letting them control you is the premise behind mindfulness. Mindfulness is a simple meditation practice that has ancient roots. You can begin by sitting, taking deep breaths, and quieting your mind or allowing your thoughts to become still. Your breath plays a big role because when you take in more oxygen by way of deeper breaths, your body relaxes and your mind becomes clearer.

Mindfulness also asks you to be fully and completely in the moment, not thinking about the past (and yes, that includes your past lives) or the future. Many mindfulness practitioners even use a mantra such as "Be here now" to remind themselves to eliminate any thoughts that are not relevant.

Forming a mindfulness habit reduces anxiety and worry and has profound health benefits. Even if you don't have a formal meditation practice, most of us can remember to stop and take a deep breath to calm our minds and renegotiate the presence of negative thoughts that are generating fear, stress, or anxiety.

TOOLS TO DEVELOP

MINDFULNESS

Mindfulness is a practice that involves quieting your mind and allowing yourself to be fully in the moment.

This means that you are not thinking about the past or the future, and you definitely are not allowing your thoughts to race so fast that they run away from you.

It is a simple concept that can be difficult to practice, let alone master.

So here is what I would like you to do: start with a few seconds at a time, maybe even just five.

Set a timer if you want.

Close your eyes, and take several deep breaths.

As you do, notice what thoughts arise.

When you do have a thought, imagine it inside a bubble and then watch it float away.

Repeat this until doing it for a few seconds becomes easy, and then slowly increase the amount of time you sit in stillness, releasing any thoughts that come until you can do it for several minutes at a time.

And so, you are doing it!

You are practicing mindfulness, and it is called a "practice" for a reason.

Another practice around learning to control your thoughts comes from yoga tradition. It involves self-inquiry, which means using your thoughts and thought patterns to learn hidden truths about yourself. Maybe you notice that you are having a thought about being late to an important meeting. That thought—*I am late*—is causing you tremendous worry and anxiety.

Through the process of self-inquiry, you might ask yourself why you need to be on time. Perhaps you conclude that the deeper truth is that you feel the need to be on time so you will be respected at work, and you are fearful that you will be regarded as less worthy of respect if you are late.

The idea is that by first noticing and then questioning your thoughts, you learn to separate them from your consciousness, which is the part of you that processes and understands life while in human form. In fact, some traditions ask you to question your own identity in relation to your thoughts: who is the "I" who is having this thought? This level of self-inquiry can be

JOURNAL TIME

SELF-INQUIRY

I want you to take a few minutes and consider one of the most recent thoughts you had.

It is best if it is a memorable or intrusive thought, or one you find yourself thinking often. Write down this thought.

Now look at that thought and ask yourself:

Is this thought true?

On what level is it true?

What deeper truth about this thought is revealed?

frustrating to some people because you gradually realize that there are always more questions you can ask about why you are having the thoughts you are having. It can even seem like one big circular conversation. But you really can excavate some inner truths about your own nature using this method.

Self-inquiry and mindfulness have existed since ancient times for a reason: because most of us have a hard time separating ourselves from our thoughts. In fact, for most people, our thoughts are so ever-present that we make the mistake of believing that we *are* our thoughts, and that our thoughts make up our consciousness.

This is not true. Your thoughts come from a place outside you. You are not your thoughts.

So where do these thoughts come from? Many come from that mysterious inner place in our minds called the unconscious. The unconscious mind is where we store our fears, our wishes and hopes, and our memories of things that have happened to us. These memories form ideas of what we can expect to happen in any given situation. Many of our memories are from this life, but some are from past lives as well.

Because our past-life memories are in our unconscious mind, they can and do influence our thoughts. In fact, they can feel as real as something that happened to you last summer, for example, even if you can't quite put your finger on when. That means you might not be able to recall the specific details of something that happened hundreds of years ago, but that memory is still influencing you and your thoughts.

Perhaps in a past life you were poor. You suffered because of

THOUGHT-PROVOKING

THE POWER OF THE UNCONSCIOUS MIND

Sigmund Freud, the early twentieth-century psychologist, believed that thoughts, behavior, and personality come from the interaction among three layers of awareness: conscious, preconscious, and unconscious.

He likened our minds to an iceberg, with the conscious (what we are aware of) being the tip, the preconscious (what can be readily accessed, such as memories or stored knowledge) being what you can see just under the surface, and the unconscious (what we are completely unaware of) being the enormous unseen bulk of the iceberg.

His theory was that the unconscious and preconscious minds play a huge role in how our lives unfold, and by accessing the unconscious and reprogramming it, we can reshape our reality.

The influence of the unconscious mind on our understanding of mental health has created an enormous shift in the fields of psychiatry and psychology, and we still are expanding our understanding of exactly how powerful it is and how much of an influence it has over our lives.

your poverty, often going hungry. You were worried or scared for your family. Maybe your child became ill, leaving you feeling helpless because you did not have the resources to get them the medicine they needed. You are likely still carrying strong feelings related to that life, like the fear of never having enough and lacking the resources to keep yourself and your family safe.

This might manifest when a situation triggers those fears or negative experiences. For example, if your credit card was declined in the grocery store, it might cause you to panic and have thoughts such as *How will I feed my family?* or *I am not safe if I can't buy this food.*

When a past-life memory is involved, any related thoughts can become magnified and might not accurately represent your present circumstances. If you're aware of the influence of a past life, instead of panicking about imminent catastrophe, you could try another credit card, call your bank to see if there was a mistake, or put a few items back on the shelf to stay within your budget.

In another example, perhaps you spend a lot of time thinking about where your husband is going and who he is talking to, and even though he has given you no reason to doubt his loyalty, you are suspicious that he is cheating on you.

When he leaves the house dressed nicely, you think he might be meeting with an affair partner, and anytime he takes a phone call in the other room, you get a sinking feeling in your stomach. In a past life, maybe your husband left you for another woman and it had devastating effects on your confidence and self-esteem. To avoid their negative influence, it's critical to recognize when you are operating from preconceptions that have nothing to do with your life now.

I once worked with a man who had been an insomniac for many years. He struggled to fall asleep every night because his thoughts would race and the anxiety from those thoughts would be so much that he simply could not drift off. His insomnia was barring him from enjoying many aspects of his life.

In his past-life experience, he recalled being a soldier who was serving as the sentinel, or night watch. He fell asleep while on duty, his regiment was attacked, and everyone was killed. He blamed himself. In this life, he still believed it was not safe to fall asleep, and that if he did, something terrible would happen. After recalling this past life, his insomnia went away. He realized that these thoughts had nothing to do with today. When he forgave himself for falling asleep all those lifetimes ago, he was able to overcome the intrusive thoughts and anxiety that had plagued him for years.

DIG DEEPER

YOUR UNCONSCIOUS PATTERNS

What are some of your own unconscious patterns?

Are any recurring thoughts influencing your life?

Causing you distress or anxiety?

Or holding you back in some way?

Thoughts come from experiences and memories, from both this life and past lives. They often are based on an unconscious belief that if something happened before, it more than likely will happen again.

A belief is a thought that has remained unexamined and, over time, has become true for us. Let's use the two previous scenarios to illustrate. If the person who was impoverished in a past life keeps having negative thoughts around their current financial situation, eventually a belief will form that "I am poor," or "There isn't enough." Over time, the suspicious wife, with her thoughts about her husband cheating, will come to a belief that "Men are cheaters," or "I am undeserving of having a loyal spouse."

Our beliefs are our truth. Just like our thoughts, our beliefs are personal. What might be true for you won't necessarily be true for someone else because they have had their own experiences and carry their own unique thoughts. Our beliefs are formed when we have similar thoughts about certain situations or people that, over time, become internalized.

People can be fierce about their beliefs. In fact, many people feel the need to defend their beliefs against others who may have opposing views. So many of us think our beliefs define us, or that who we are is based on what we believe.

These self-defining beliefs can be about ourselves, religion or spirituality, institutions, companies, groups or affiliations, or other individuals. They come from experiences we have had in both this life and past lives. But just like our thoughts, our beliefs are not *us*. They come from a place outside us. They are not who we are.

Years ago, I worked with a man who had been single for many years and, despite saying that he wanted to marry and have a family, he was a bachelor well into his forties. He was a handsome, charismatic veterinarian with his own practice and in every way was considered a good catch.

In our first session, he described his relationship pattern: he meets a woman; finds her attractive; takes her on several dates; and then, when he feels like she is getting "too close" (his words), he focuses on either a real or perceived flaw and breaks up with her. He even admitted to breaking up with a woman because he didn't like how she pulled on her ear when she was nervous.

He also believed that "women aren't worth the trouble" and "ladies will just end up breaking your heart"—unconscious thoughts that had crystallized into beliefs he had carried for so long they were true for him. In his past life, he remembered being in 1800s Ireland as a husband to a woman whom he loved deeply. She became ill and died young, leaving him feeling helpless and overwhelmed by his grief and sadness.

He now saw that his beliefs about women were based on an unconscious fear of falling in love and then suffering a loss and heartbreak. He could see that his relationship patterns were based on this fear and that he was sabotaging himself by not allowing himself to get to know any woman beyond a surface level. After he opened himself to the possibility of true intimacy and love, along with the potential pain at losing that love, he met his future wife within a year. He told me he isn't sure if she is the same woman whom he had loved before but it "felt like it did with her."

His unconscious thoughts had become beliefs that were holding him back from finding true love, and after he was able to unravel those beliefs and see that they were not based on reality, love found him pretty quickly. He just had to get out of his own way and let go of the false and self-destructive beliefs that his unconscious thoughts had formed.

REVISIONIST HISTORY

EXAMINING YOUR BELIEFS

Take a few minutes and write down some of your most deeply held beliefs.

I want you to place them into categories: beliefs about myself, beliefs about my spouse or family, beliefs about my community, my spiritual beliefs, beliefs about my country or political beliefs, beliefs about certain religions or groups or minorities, and beliefs about the world at large.

Feel free to add any other category you feel drawn to.

What are these beliefs? Where did they come from?

Some of our beliefs are inherited from our family of origin or influenced by our culture or background. Others are based on direct experience.

Look at your list of beliefs and consider their roots. How did you form those beliefs?

Now, let's talk about the concept of truth. Many of our beliefs become true—*for us*. It is important to remember that truth is a personal concept, and what might be true for you isn't necessarily true for someone else. There is no such thing as truth in a universal sense; it varies from person to person.

When we have a fixed set of ideologies and belief systems and are overly attached to the concept of our own truth, we are blind to seeing others' viewpoints. When we begin to change the way we look at our thoughts and beliefs to understand that they are based on our unique experiences, we can also transform the way we approach truth. We create our truths during many lives and, in fact, one of the biggest opportunities we have in any lifetime is to find our own truth. But that truth doesn't need to be fixed. Truth is fluid, constantly changing, and we must be flexible, too.

Many people have told me they don't believe in past lives, which makes complete sense if they have never experienced their own. It is one thing to believe that something exists or is possible and another to experience it directly. Then, that belief becomes your own, found truth.

By approaching your unique truth in this way, it is easier to have compassion for others who might not share your beliefs. When you encounter another person who has a different found truth, you can learn to see that as a product of their thoughts and beliefs that have come by way of their experiences. If both of you have a truth that is your own, then what is there to argue about?

When you realize that you are not your thoughts or beliefs, you can control them rather than allowing them to dictate your experience. You can reframe how and why these thoughts occur by examining where they come from: the memories from the past and present that formed them.

Consider your beliefs as crystallized thoughts. What you see is true and unique to you and you alone. Remember, your thoughts or beliefs, as well as your individual truth, are fluid concepts. This means that you can always shift your thoughts, as well as your beliefs, to match a new experience.

MEDITATION MOMENT

Find a comfortable place to sit where you won't be distracted, and close your eyes.

Take a few deep breaths, and allow your body to relax.

As you settle, notice your thoughts.

Try not to attach to these thoughts, but if something comes into your mind, notice what you are thinking about.

Keep taking deep breaths, and keep noticing your thoughts as they come.

There's no need to stop or block these thoughts. Instead, pull yourself into a place of observation and watch your thoughts arise.

Now, choose one thought that you would like to explore.

For example, is there something that has been weighing on your heart?

Are you worried or concerned about someone or something?

Are you thinking about an upcoming event?

Ask yourself:

What is the source of this thought?

Is it something that has happened before?

Or are you worried about a potential future outcome?

Try to stay in the space of being an observer.
Now ask yourself:

What is the source of this thought?

How is it taking you away from being in the present moment?

Have you connected a belief to this thought?

For now, there is no need to actually answer these questions—again, you are just observing.

Whenever you become aware of the fact that you are having this thought, tell yourself, "I am having this thought."

Now, I want you to ask yourself who is the "I" who is having this thought.

Stay in this space for a few moments, and allow your answer to come without judgment.

Slowly open your eyes, and pick up your journal.

What beliefs do you hold that are connected to this thought?

For example, if your thought was about world peace, what belief do you have around that?

Do you believe world peace is possible?

If your thought was about your partner or your child, what related beliefs do you hold?

Now that you have discovered how your thoughts and beliefs are connected, what are some of the beliefs you hold that you would like to challenge?

Do you have beliefs that are based on fear, prejudice, or negative experiences?

What thoughts are connected to those beliefs? When you change your thoughts, do you notice that your beliefs change, too?

six

YOU ARE NOT
YOUR RELATIONSHIPS OR ROLES

One of the things that defines our experience in a human body is how we relate to others. We are naturally social creatures, and it is not in our nature to be alone. We all crave connection and intimacy as part of our basic needs. Touch, communication, protection, and a sense of belonging are important to everyone.

Now, obviously people differ on their preferred level of sociability depending on factors such as personality and environment, but suffice it to say that our need to relate to others in meaningful ways is stitched into our DNA and without it, we literally would not survive.

Because we have an inherent drive to have meaningful interactions with others, we end up being in various types of relationships throughout our lifetime. Through those relationships, we also play various roles in order to meet our social and emotional needs. We are husbands, wives, mothers, fathers, sisters, daughters, brothers, sons, neighbors, friends, lovers, teachers, students, employers, employees—each of these describes a relationship but also comes with certain expectations for the role you are meant to play within that dynamic.

We are born into a family, a community, and instinctively are drawn to being a part of a group or a pair. Yes, this instinct serves an important biological purpose, including protection and procreation, but it also is something we crave on a deep, spiritual level. We want to belong, feel loved, and have a sense of connection with other people.

Not every family or community provides that sense of belonging or safety. Some parents are not emotionally equipped to step into the role of parent. Many of us experience the loss of that much-needed circle of intimacy through death, divorce, mental illness, drug addiction, poverty, or displacement. Many of us suffer from not having enough people in our lives who care about us, who nourish and protect us. But even for those of us who did not grow up in a traditional family, the need and desire to live in community is inherent and will drive us to seek out that social and emotional sustenance elsewhere. Many of us have friends who are "like family," marry a spouse who fills the gap left by a lack of parental support, or have neighbors who drop by to say hello and bring us food when we are sick. We need each other.

I have discovered that the connections you form with other people do not always come about because you met or crossed paths with them in this life. Instead, they often originate in a past life you shared together. You are drawn to the same people over and over again, and your connection has profound meaning and purpose. Upon reuniting in this life, you already have a robust foundation that can be built upon and expanded now and in the future.

If you are willing to look, you will discover that there is a spiritual level to all of our relationships, which comes from the history we have shared. These are your soulmates.

In all of the years I have been doing past-life work, by far the topic that carries the most interest and fascination is the idea of soulmates. We all want to know who our soulmates are, how we can meet them if we are single, and how to excavate our past-life history with someone else. The notion of a soulmate is incredibly romantic—the idea that you loved someone before, and even after being separated by death, you have found each other again across oceans of time.

A lot of stereotypes exist about soulmates, most of which revolve around the idea that they are romantic in nature or centered around a life partner or spouse. But we have many soulmates, of many different types. In fact, I have come to define the term as anyone you have known before, in a past life. This means that your list of potential soulmates is likely quite long. And because you haven't always looked like you do now, or had the same gender, ethnicity, etc., you haven't always shown up in relationship with a specific person in the same way. That's what makes it so interesting.

I have had the privilege of witnessing many clients experience past lives, and I have come to learn that soulmates are very real. We do reunite with loved ones whom we have known before. It is always incredible to me how the universe conspires to bring together two people who are meant to meet. You could be born on the other side of the world from someone with whom you have shared a past life and "just happen" to bump into each other on the street.

I absolutely love soulmate stories. Yes, I am a hopeless romantic, but how can I resist when so often there is a sprinkle of magic involved in the way two people who have known each other before meet again in this life? It is just so delightful and inspiring. Often a coincidence or synchronicity is involved, such as a missed train, a sudden rainstorm, or a canceled flight that charted the course of their eventual meeting.

I hear soulmates describe discovering interesting or unusual things they have in common, such as sharing their mothers' birthday. I have even heard of soulmates who have had the same group of friends for years but never met, or had the feeling that they had just missed each other several times before they actually met. I once worked with a woman who was employed in the same office building as her now husband for years before they met much later on a blind date.

And again, soulmates are not just romantic. Someone once told me that when they met their future mother-in-law, she seemed familiar, like they knew her already. Or that they met their best friend when they accidentally fell down the stairs and a stranger stopped to help them. Or that they saw their future child in a dream, years before they were born.

We have many soulmates and can and do meet new ones all the time. The idea that a soulmate is only applicable to a romantic partner creates a false notion that there is one person out there for us, and that's who we are looking for. Many people tell

THOUGHT-PROVOKING

What are some of your soulmate stories?

How did you meet some of the most important people in your life?

Upon first meeting them, did they seem familiar somehow?

Were there any coincidences, or did your meeting seem meant to be?

me they are single because they are searching for that perfect partner, the person who will complete them. This is a fallacy in part because no one is "incomplete," but also because this idea prevents people from seeing and recognizing the soulmate who is in front of them, right now.

This overidealization of soulmates is encapsulated in terms such as *twin flame* and *twin soul*, which imply that your other half is out there, also looking for you. This notion comes from the writings of Plato, the ancient Greek philosopher. In his work *Symposium*, he describes a legend in which the god Zeus decided to split human beings into two halves. These splintered pieces were doomed to spend many lifetimes searching for each other, longing to be whole again. According to the story, Zeus did this because he was afraid of our power as human beings and wanted to diminish it to maintain control over us.

I have found that there are almost as many possible soulmates out there for us as there are choices in life. When we are in a real partnership, we are not just twice as strong but exponentially so. We are not looking for our match, but rather our *complement*. In order to find that complement, though, we first have to learn how to be "enough" on our own. Looking for someone to complete you will not guide you to a true partnership in the same way that cultivating yourself and standing on your own will.

Think about your many potential romantic soulmates like a deck of cards: The deck holds a lot of different cards, all of which represent possible life partners. Some will be electric and exciting, and some will be grounded and stable. Some come with difficult lessons, while others are evolved and loving. When a relationship ends and you decide to part ways with a soulmate, the deck shuffles again and allows for the possibility of meeting another of these many potential partners.

Again, there is no such thing as "the one," and not all soulmate relationships are romantic. They can be, and your soulmate could be your loving partner or spouse, but they could also be your family, friends, coworkers, and even your enemies. In fact, I suspect that all of the significant people around you, both the loving and supportive relationships and the difficult ones that are fraught with challenges, are soulmates who have reincarnated with you.

All relationships come with challenges. Even the most loving and present parent; the most giving spouse; or the sweet, adoring child can, well, get on our nerves. But those conflicts and tensions often have the most to teach us. Many of the key lessons in life come from our dealings with other people, and navigating these relationships consciously is a powerful vehicle for

TOOLS TO DEVELOP

HOW TO RECOGNIZE A SOULMATE

How do you know if someone is your soulmate?

Here are some clues for recognizing a soulmate when you meet them:

* They seem familiar somehow, or you feel that you may have met them before (but haven't in this life).

* You feel recognition when you look into their eyes. The eyes are the windows to the soul, and you can sense a deep, soul-level connection when you gaze into the eyes of a soulmate.

* A certain quality in their voice resonates with you. Many people describe feeling drawn to a soulmate's voice when they are speaking or singing.

* You experience a déjà vu sensation around them or realize that you saw them in a dream.

* Your paths have *almost* crossed before.

* You have strange, even random things in common.

* Meeting them felt important or fated.

self-growth. Being honest and open, learning to give and receive love equally, and allowing the other person to be a mirror and reflect your own places in need of growth is a compelling spiritual practice.

Given how vital our interpersonal relationships are, it isn't

JOURNAL TIME

Take a moment to think about the important people in your life.

This should include people who might have already passed or are not present.

Try to put them into some categories.

Some will be in more than one category. For those who are not present, focus on who they were when they were on this plane with you.

In your journal, make a list of the people who are easy to relate to, naturally loving, and supportive. These people are the most helpful, reliable, and dependable.

Now, make another list of the people in your life who are challenging to relate to. Feel free to include why you feel this way.

I want you to look at both lists.

These are your soulmates. Even the challenging ones.

surprising that many of us look at them as a part of our identity and who we think we are. We've all heard the idea that one can lose oneself in a bad relationship, implying that there is codependency involved or pressure to change aspects of your habits or personality to make the relationship work. But on a simpler level, how many times have you been tempted to answer the question "Who are you?" with a relationship or role? "I am a father." "I am a boss." "I am a teacher." "I am a girlfriend." And so on.

When we look at our relationships through the lens of past lives, we quickly realize that defining who we are by way of our relationships is another false identity. In previous lives, we were not those roles and did not have the same relationships. We lived in a different time and place, with a different name, appearance, and gender.

MEDITATION MOMENT

Take a moment to sit, close your eyes, and take a few deep breaths.

I want you to focus on a specific relationship you have; just choose the first one that comes to mind.

As you sit and breathe deeply, contemplate:

How does this relationship make me feel?

What needs are met for me in the context of this relationship?

How do I meet the other person's needs?

How can I honor the relationship more?

We are not our relationships, but that doesn't mean those relationships haven't been integral parts of our current and previous lives. I am willing to bet that your list of soulmates includes people who play distinct roles in your day-to-day—not just your partner or spouse, but your parents, grandparents, children, siblings, cousins, friends, coworkers or boss, and maybe even your favorite server at your local diner. The fact that these people come from your past lives, and you have a backstory to each relationship, helps explain why some of them are easier to get along with than others.

Perhaps you have a sibling with whom you always argue over who does more to help your elderly parents, calling each other selfish and fighting over who is more dependable. But maybe in a past life, you and your sibling had to compete for resources that were vital to your survival, such as food or water. That dynamic endures in your relationship today, as you trigger that competitiveness in each other, and now you are meant to discover how to better share responsibilities and give way to the needs of your sibling while also helping your parents.

Or you may have a best friend with whom you have never fought, over anything, and the two of you seem to innately understand and love each other. This could be because she was your mother in a past life, and that unconditional love she had for you has carried over. Her presence today is a gift that teaches you what this type of love looks like in another context. Remember, you are here, reincarnated in another body, to learn lessons. Those lessons are about love in its many forms.

We play roles for each other—mother, friend, employee, sister, grandfather, engineer, president, baseball player, teammate. Depending on the culture and time period, each comes with certain expectations.

A mother is often expected to be nurturing, to care for children, and to be maternal, which implies that there are certain innate qualities to this role. A husband is expected to be the provider, protector, hunter, and warrior. Even if we feel like the roles are antiquated, the expectations remain.

When I was a child, one of my family's favorite things to play on game night was Old Maid. The deck contained an odd number of cards, and every card had a match except one—the one with a picture of a dowdy-looking older woman wearing a comfy sweater with a cat on her lap. This was the Old Maid, and the loser of the game was the one who was left holding this card. It was just a card game, but it upheld a stereotype about women who reach a "certain age" and are still unmarried. To be an old maid means being the leftovers, the undesired, and that without a partner, a woman doesn't have a place in society. It implies that without the role of "wife," she isn't living the full expression of who she should be.

Even in our more enlightened society however many decades later, as gender roles and expectations shift, it doesn't change the fact that, for example, your child needs what might be called "mothering" by someone who exhibits the expected maternal traits.

It is so hard to push back against our various roles and the way we are in relationships with others. After all, we are social creatures, and being in relationships is one of our deepest needs. Some of the roles we play naturally demand a certain amount of selflessness, as you shelve your own wants, needs, and desires in deference to another. If that role is one of caregiver or nurturer, it can be particularly difficult not to dissolve your sense of self as you fulfill the role.

Our roles and relationships are not fixed; they are constantly changing. A woman who has been married for forty years might find herself widowed and mourning not only the death of her spouse but also her identity as a wife. A single father who has raised four kids on his own might discover that, after they leave home, he doesn't know who he is outside that all-encompassing role. A dedicated employee who works nights and weekends,

DIG DEEPER

I want you to spend some time thinking about the various ways you show up for others in your life.

What roles do you play?

How have these roles shaped your identity?

putting her career above her personal life, finds herself laid off or unemployed—what now? Defining who we are based on our roles or relationships is not the whole story. Natural shifts and changes over time make them shaky ground upon which to build an identity.

Not only that, but the roles you occupy now and the nature of your various relationships have not always been the same. We can and do change roles with each other over many lifetimes. Relationships are about learning and growing. If we kept passing through identical lives, we wouldn't be maximizing our potential for growth in these relationships. Your daughter in this life may have been your mother in a past life. Your spouse could have been your parent, your friend, your boss, your sibling—you get it. We are here to learn about love from many angles: romantic love, familial love, motherly love, friendship, admiration, obsession (which is a toxic form of love), and self-love. They are all love.

It might seem strange that a relationship that feels so central and specific once might have featured a totally different type of love. I have seen many clients discover that their loved ones today have been with them before, and even though they are initially surprised at the shift in dynamic, ultimately, they say it makes a certain kind of sense.

I once worked with a woman who saw that her six-year-old son had been her husband, and her husband had been her brother. She laughed and said that her son displayed protective instincts toward her and was in tune with her emotional needs, and her husband was her best friend and "favorite drinking buddy." It was clear that some residue of their old dynamics had carried over.

I often see soulmates in patterns as well because they need more than one lifetime to work out the lesson or challenge that their relationship is presenting. A couple can be married many times across many lives but swap genders or roles, such as who is the breadwinner or the homemaker. Or a mother and daughter may switch, taking turns as the parent to forge a multidimensional understanding of each other in that specific context.

Our relationships with our various soulmates are a gift. They are sacred in that we made agreements with each other, or soul contracts that stipulate how we will show up for each other in each lifetime and present a certain lesson, which may be about recognizing and receiving love.

Our difficult relationships are a gift as well, even if they don't feel like it. I am sure you can look at a rocky relationship and realize both its influence on your learning and growth and the role it played in your becoming the person you are today. Hindsight always brings clarity.

Remember that our roles and relationships are mutable, so if you think that who you are has anything to do with your current dynamic with another person, think again. You are not your relationships, and you are not defined by the roles you play. You have been mothers, fathers, grandparents, and children.

You have also had lives in which you have not been married or had children, and some in which you had a big family or community, and you found your identity in each in other ways. Although the key people in your life—your soulmates—play a crucial role in meeting your needs as a human being and are some of your greatest teachers, they do not define you, either.

Remember, the most important relationship you will ever have is the one you have with yourself.

REVISIONIST HISTORY
SHIFTING ROLES WITH YOUR SOULMATES

For this exercise, I want you to pick one person with whom you are in a relationship. This can be anyone, from your spouse to your neighbor down the street.

Go with the first person who comes to mind. You can do this exercise as many times as you like, but for now, just pick one person to focus on.

Think about your relationship. Who are you to them, and who are they to you? What roles do you play for each other?

Now imagine that person in a different role or relationship. Choose one that is less intimate than the one you are in now.

For example, if you are mother and daughter, imagine that

you are sisters who live across the country from each other. Or if you are spouses, imagine that you are friends or coworkers.

I want you to really sit with this new dynamic and make up a story about how you interact with each other.

What do you talk about?

How much time do you spend together?

What needs do you fill for each other?

Now repeat the exercise, but this time, make the relationship more intimate, even closer. If you are married, imagine that you are twins. If you are twins, imagine that you are married.

What does this relationship feel like?

What is expected of you in this relationship?

What do you expect to get back?

seven

YOU ARE NOT
YOUR SUFFERING

One of the things about life we know we can count on is that each of us will have our share of challenges and struggles. Dealing with situations that are painful or disappointing is inevitable.

We all experience loss, illness, the deaths of loved ones, tragedy, and disasters. These painful events often are completely out of our control, which can add a feeling of helplessness to the emotional hurt.

Life is filled with joy and beauty, yet life is also about suffering. Even though some of us seem to skate by mostly unscathed, no one is immune. It isn't fair, either, the way challenges are doled out. One person lives to middle age without ever having lost a loved one, while their neighbor experienced the death of a close family member at an early age. Or someone is fortunate enough to have found a loving partner in college, while another is still alone in their fifties, searching for and longing for that kind of love and support. Some people are lucky to have robust health, while others have chronic illnesses that plague them for years.

I have known people who have dealt with one challenge after another and wonder why. Why is their life far more difficult than others'? How is it fair that they have to deal with so much?

As a child, I struggled a lot with the concept of fairness. How could life be so kind to some and so cruel to others? I thought about how some babies die in infancy, while some people live to be one hundred. Some are lucky to have strong bodies, while others lose their ability to walk in a car accident. Why are some people born rich and well cared for and others into extreme poverty or to parents who cannot provide them with the love they need and deserve? Why do bad things happen to good, kind, loving people?

I grew up in a family that didn't believe in reincarnation, or even know what the concept was, so I wondered: If we have one life and, therefore, only one chance to experience all there is, how could such unfairness exist?

It wasn't until I discovered reincarnation—that we *don't* just have this one existence and one chance to experience the joy and fullness of what life in a human body has to offer—that I was able to reconcile this seeming injustice. Finding out that there is so much more than this one lifetime helped me open a curtain to a larger view. Sometimes we are given one challenge and not another; sometimes we get an "easier" life or one that features a lot of struggle and pain.

What is it all for, then? Why do we have to experience these rougher aspects of life? Why can't we all just have lives that are easy and filled with joy? What purpose do these challenges serve? I have come to believe that the hard knocks we experience are how we learn and grow. We struggle through hardships, pain, and suffering because of what these teach us. This is not easy, but this is how we grow.

The growth from these experiences comes via the way we endure or handle these challenges, by how we step up and decide to work through them. This is how we gain wisdom—even if sometimes in a trial by fire. Because we learn by doing, we need to have firsthand experiences in order to really absorb the lessons. This is the "why" of reincarnation, the point of returning to Earth in a new body again and again: we want to evolve and grow.

And guess what? You chose to be here, and you chose to take on the specific challenges of your life.

I know that can be a difficult idea to process, especially if you're in the darkness of a particularly painful time. But our lives have a kind of master plan that was decided before we were born. Through my clients' experiences, I have come to learn that there is a process that happens after we die that can best be described as a life review. After transitioning from a body back to a spirit, we spend time contemplating the life we just lived, looking at the events that happened and considering the choices we made. We examine where we succeeded in being kind, loving, gentle, and helpful, and where we could have done better and made different, more loving choices.

What is especially interesting is that people describe this afterlife period with remarkable consistency. They also note that the review process is self-driven and not what many imagine based on a judgment-day stereotype, during which you are shamed and punished for any misdeeds you committed. The process is much more compassionate than that.

At the end of the day, it is up to each of us to look at our lives and decide what we could do better. We look at what our goals were at the outset and how well we achieved them. Based on what we still need to learn and experience, we then make a plan for the next life that includes all of the challenges and struggles we decide to take on.

After this life review, we plan our next incarnation based on what we wish we had done differently and the lessons we still need to master. During this process we often consult with our spirit guides, who have wisdom and perspective we do not. We decide where we will be born, who our parents will be, the location and circumstances of that lifetime, and the struggles we will endure. (That said, once reborn, we have free will and nothing is predetermined about how we will *respond* to strife. How we handle our struggles is the big test of the school of life we keep reincarnating into, with the hopes of graduating to the next grade.)

Many people ask me, "When does it end? When have I learned enough that can I stop reincarnating?" The truth is, I don't think it ever ends. Everything in nature exists in never-ending cycles of life, death, and rebirth. As a part of nature ourselves, why would we be any different? No matter how much we learn, grow, and evolve, there is always more to know and ways we can become better, wiser, more loving beings.

I once worked with a woman who had suffered through an

A LITTLE DIRECTION

WHAT IS A SPIRIT GUIDE?

We all have spirit guides, or beings who are in spirit, not incarnated, and around us at all times.

They know what is happening in our lives; love and care about us; and give us insight, information, and guidance when we need it.

They often are the source of coincidences or synchronicities, can facilitate when and how we meet a soulmate, and help us through challenging seasons.

They can and do include our ancestors who have passed: parents, grandparents or great-grandparents, aunts and uncles, and siblings.

They also include friends and people who we knew, loved, and were connected to.

Spirit guides can also be people we knew in a past life who are on the other side.

Others are teachers, mentors, and wise beings who have achieved a higher level of learning and evolution than we have and guide us based on their earned knowledge and understanding. Some people refer to these types of spirit guides as angels, archangels, ascended masters, and master spirits.

All of these spirit guides can and do guide us, whether we knew them in this life or not.

extremely abusive childhood. Both of her parents were emotionally ill-equipped to have a child and also regularly abused drugs. Her father was violent—once to the point of breaking her bones, an incident that resulted in child services removing her from her home, only to place her with emotionally neglectful and abusive foster parents.

She had a vivid past-life experience, after which she met with her spirit guides and realized that having those specific parents led her to treat her own children with kindness, love, and nurturing. She had triumphed in moving through her traumatic circumstances to become the person and parent she is today.

THOUGHT-PROVOKING

WHAT ARE YOUR BIGGEST CHALLENGES?

Take a few minutes to think about your life so far.

What have been your biggest challenges?

How have you dealt with them?

What are some of the lessons these challenges have taught you?

Now, my goal is never to tell someone who is going through a challenging time that they chose it, implying that they should suck it up. Each of our paths is unique, and the choices another has made, on this plane or another, are not for us to judge. When in doubt, we must always show compassion and love for our fellow humans because they grapple with life just as we do.

Many of our toughest times can result in trauma, which presents complex challenges for many years or an entire lifetime. Symptoms may not show up for a while but then linger for years, impacting body, mind, and spirit. A traumatic event can shatter your sense of the world as you understand it and rob you of your sense of safety and security.

Symptoms of post-traumatic stress disorder (PTSD) include anxiety, intrusive thoughts and images, flashbacks, nightmares, and disturbed sleep, as well as panic attacks, hypervigilance, depression, numbness, and avoidant behavior such as abusing alcohol or drugs.

Trauma and its lasting effects should be taken seriously, when looking at their impact both in your life and in the lives of others. If any of these descriptions feels familiar, take time to acknowledge what you've been through, give yourself the space and time to process it, and seek out a qualified mental health professional to guide you through the often painful and arduous work of healing.

Trauma comes from events that you can trace to this life, but symptoms of trauma can come from a past life as well. Years ago, I worked with a woman whose therapist had diagnosed her with PTSD. She had panic attacks and was anxious to the point of being afraid to leave her house, which was clearly impacting her quality of life. But what was most troubling for her was that she could not remember any specific traumatic event that would have affected her in such a profound way.

Because many of her anxious feelings centered around her two young children, her therapist thought that perhaps her PTSD stemmed from the difficult or traumatic birth of one of them, which she had buried in her unconscious. She considered this, but because neither birth was necessarily difficult, she still couldn't quite get to the root cause to deal with her feelings in a way that would allow her to heal. Still, her emotional response to the trauma was very real indeed.

When we worked together, she had a vivid past-life experience as a woman in eighteenth-century France who had her children violently taken from her. She realized that her PTSD was from that life, not this one.

Her therapist was partially right, then, because becoming a mother and giving birth to her children had triggered her previous trauma to emerge from her unconscious. After she realized where her fear around losing her children came from, her PTSD symptoms went away entirely.

I also worked with a woman who displayed symptoms of sexual abuse. She could not recall what she had endured, but it is common for victims of abuse to bury traumatic memories to protect themselves. Her therapist thought it was possible that the triggering event had occurred early in her childhood. The process of trying to get to the bottom of what had happened to her nearly tore her family apart.

Then, during a session with me, she discovered that she had, in fact, suffered from sexual abuse—in a past life. This is one reason it is vital always to believe victims and honor the feelings that come up. The unconscious mind is a deep ocean that contains memories from both this life and past ones.

It is possible to experience past-life trauma as vividly and emotionally resonant as anything that has happened in this life. Sometimes it is both, and the trauma from your past life is just another layer underneath your experienced trauma in this life.

But despite the trauma we have endured, we human beings are strong and resilient. Through the years, I have come to realize how much suffering so many of us have endured—*and* how many of us still manage to survive, thrive, and move forward in a powerful and meaningful way.

When you look at your past lives and specific past-life memories, one of the things that will jump out at you is how difficult some of your experiences were. You don't have to be a historian to know that human beings have undergone hardships of many types across many millennia. Chances are, we all encountered war, plague, enslavement, torture, murder, persecution, betrayal, famine, floods, and starvation.

When you understand that you have been given these extreme challenges before, and your soul has successfully overcome them, you can reframe the way you approach any adversity you are dealing with today. You already are battle-tested. You can feel empowered based on what you have endured and the wisdom you have worked so hard to gain.

Perhaps you have lost your job and are worried about how you will be able to afford your bills and support your family. You also are aware that in a past life you were homeless, living in extreme poverty, and ultimately died from hunger because you had no support system and lived in a small village where there were no opportunities for work. You did your best given the circumstances, but you did not succeed in surviving that misfortune.

Even though you did not survive in that life, you were able to bring the wisdom you gained with you into this one, as well as the knowledge that you have encountered a similar situation before and some things have changed for the better. Today, you are educated and can more easily move towns or cities for a job, and many more industries are available that might launch a new career for you.

You realize that even though losing your job is stressful, you will find another one eventually. For now, you have a roof over your head. Your past lives give new insight and perspective that you may have had it worse before, giving you a chance to focus on the blessings of your life today.

They say what doesn't kill you makes you stronger. Well, sometimes it did kill you. Sometimes what you endured caused your past life to end. But you can still use the experiences from that life to gain wisdom today. So it can still make you stronger.

DIG DEEPER

Take a minute and, without attaching to them too much, make a list of the things in your life that have caused you suffering.

It can be anything that comes to mind—a small incident or a large issue.

Write down what comes to mind without analyzing or judging it yet.

Now, when you have a list (of any length), take a minute to think about the person you were before the event that caused this suffering. Write down two or three words that come to mind that describe this former version of you.

Think about who you became after this event, the person you were after you experienced this suffering.

Write down some words that describe that person who survived those difficult or painful challenges.

What do you notice? How did you change?

We've touched on the unfairness of why some people struggle more than others, or why bad things happen to good people, which is connected to the concept of karma. Karma is the idea that your deeds in life, whether good or bad, dictate the terms of your next incarnation. That is, if you are not a good person in this life, you will be punished in the next by encountering more pain and struggles than you would have otherwise. I have found that this is not entirely true; the process is more complicated than that.

Karma is a Sanskrit word that means "action," which implies that we are in control of the energy we are creating around our lives and our choices. Karma is not something we "get" but rather is a direct result of our actions. You may have heard it paired with the words *good* and *bad*—that is, doing something kind or generous gives us "good karma," which earns us a reward in the next life, while "bad karma" is something we fear, with its underlying threat of punishment.

One of the most common fears I encounter among my clients is the idea that by uncovering past-life memories, they will discover that they were a "terrible person" in a past life. The concept that you might not like yourself or the things you did can become a hindrance to fully opening to this process. I try to explain that we all have made mistakes. Remember, the entire point of being here is to learn and grow.

Karma is not about punishment. I do believe that "the good you do comes back to you," meaning that if you are a loving, kind person, you will attract certain gifts and opportunities based on that vibe. But many good people still face hard times, while selfish, mean, bigoted people lead charmed lives. That's why you should never judge anyone based on what you imagine their karma is.

Those among us who have made it to the other side of some enormous challenges often seem to be happier, are wiser, and possess a strength of character others do not. They are able to take not only a giant step forward in their spiritual growth and development, but an enormous leap in their soul's evolution. Suffering, meanwhile, is often caused by the way we view or handle our challenges. Perhaps your beloved pet has just died after a long illness. Of course, you are devastated, but you have a choice to focus on the wonderful memories you had together or bury yourself in grief. Or perhaps you have received a scary diagnosis from your doctor. Your health is on the line, and perhaps even your life. Will you give up, deciding to be angry, depressed, and withdrawn about the unfairness of it all? Or will you follow your doctor's advice to the letter, do your own research about your condition to find out if any lifestyle changes might maximize your healing potential, and tackle the challenge with a positive attitude?

You always have a choice. Sometimes it is not about what life throws your way, but about how you respond. Struggles are not optional; they are mandatory, and there is no way around them. But how they impact you is of your own design.

I'm not trying to be flippant about the ease of shifting your perspective on these kinds of personal catastrophes. I have experienced deaths in my family, divorce, financial struggles, disappointment, and heartbreak. Like everyone, I have suffered. Removing yourself from suffering by accepting life's challenges as the ones *you* chose before you were born is not something most of us can do. It can take many lifetimes to accept the truth that there is a bigger picture to existence and that suffering is optional, even in the darkest of moments.

If we all had mastered this, we would not be here, slogging through this school of life. If we look around, we might see that some of our fellow humans are farther along the path than we are. Some people have already reincarnated many times and have had a lot of past lives, earning wisdom through experience. You may have heard the term *old soul*, but I don't believe that age guarantees wisdom. You can be old and still be ignorant quite easily. I prefer to use the term *evolved soul* to describe people who have been here many times before, figured out some important things about life and how best to live it, and put in the time and effort to maximize their potential for growth.

Suffering does not define you. When you look across your lives, you can take inspiration from what you have come through. This perspective does not make your challenges go away, but when you realize that there is a purpose to your suffering, and that your soul has chosen this path, you no longer need to allow this suffering to become your identity. It is only today's battle, and you have fought and won before, in many places and in many times.

JOURNAL TIME

I want you to take out your journal.

Take a moment to choose a specific challenge that you have. It can be something you are dealing with currently or something you struggled with in the past.

Go with the first thing that comes to mind, without overthinking it.

Ask yourself:

What made that situation challenging? How did it make you feel?

How did you handle it? What happened?

How did it resolve, or are you working toward resolving it?

Now, I want you to randomly choose a number between one and ten thousand. Let it be the first number that comes to you. That number is now the year you are in.

When you decide on a date, you can choose whether the year is BCE or CE, but I want you to make sure that it is a time that occurred in the past, not the future.

For example, if you chose 500, that can be either 1,500 years ago or 2,500 years ago.

Now, really be there.

What do you know about what was happening in the world at that time?

What was life like back then?

Now, imagine that you are dealing with that same challenge you picked at the start of this exercise, only during the year you chose.

What would be different about it? What would change?

How does being in that time period change how you look at that challenge?

What elements of your struggle are universal and would be true in any time period?

eight

YOU ARE NOT
YOUR "STORY"

Years ago, I traveled to Taos, New Mexico, to seek out a Cherokee medicine woman I wanted to meet.

It had been a rough couple years—I got divorced, became a single mother to two children who were still in diapers, moved across the country, and lost my beloved grandmother.

I wanted to learn from the medicine woman, but I also wanted to be healed.

I am not sure what I expected her to be like, although I may have had some New Age stereotypes in mind. Because she was "spiritual," I imagined that she would be warm and loving, inviting me into her arms and healing me with her gentle embrace.

When I opened the door, though, a gruff-looking woman with black, darting eyes like a crow pushed past me and pointed to a chair. I sat.

She stared at me intently, ignoring my discomfort at the lack of pleasantries, and asked, "Why are you here?"

I began stammering my tale of woe—who I am, the heartbreak I had suffered, the traumatic events of the past couple years.

Midway through my first sentence, she got up abruptly and waved her hand impatiently in front of my face.

"That is a really boring story," she said. "Do you think you are the only one who has a story?"

My jaw dropped in disbelief. As I sat there, dumbfounded, she continued, "If you keep telling that story, then it will keep following you around."

It didn't take me long to figure out that she was right. It was a really boring story. And because I kept telling it, I kept making it true. Not only was it following me around, but I had come to identify with it. As long as I continued to tell it, it was going to be mine.

Over time, I learned a lot from this wise medicine woman and realized that despite my initial judgment, she was extraordinarily gentle, kind, and loving. I had created a story about her, too—a preconceived idea about who I thought she should be instead of who she was.

The stories we tell about ourselves and others have power, in that by continuing to tell them, we allow them to manifest and continue to be true. The situations and circumstances of our lives follow suit, based on this ongoing narrative.

The stories we tell about ourselves and others are formed by attitudes, beliefs, prejudices, and preconceived ideas, not what's actually in front of us. Our personal narrative is often based on deep feelings about who we believe ourselves to be and what we feel we *should* want, need, and deserve.

We all have a story to tell. In fact, telling stories is how we express our identity, highlights how we present ourselves to others, and may be an unconscious response or a mask we are used to wearing. Our stories include our name, looks, background, social status, career, and the roles we play within our family and society. We naturally want to characterize ourselves in a way that emphasizes that we are unique and interesting. It is human nature to categorize ourselves and others so we understand where we belong in the social order.

It is through storytelling that we can connect to another person via their description of how they show up in the world. And it helps us understand and process information about each other in a way that is relatable and memorable.

How do you respond when someone asks, "Who are you?" You might think of your name and a few physical traits or

THOUGHT-PROVOKING

WHAT IS YOUR STORY?

What is your story?

How do you tell it?

Spend a few minutes thinking about the stories you tell about yourself.

What elements do you include?

characteristics to respond with, like tall, short, skinny, curvy, curly haired, balding, blue-eyed, or brunette. Maybe you include features of your personality, such as funny, smart, shy, or outspoken. Or your answer might include your job and the roles you play, such as a lawyer, teacher, mother of three, mechanic, brother-in-law, husband, or cook. This is all part of your story.

Often we become attached to this story, and our identity hardens around it. When asked, "Who are you?" these would be understandable responses: "I am a Clevelander," "I am a teacher," "I am a wife and mother who is battling cancer," or "I am a thirty-year-old Asian American man who has just lost my job." These are all stories.

Some of the stories we tell are about things we feel are positive, such as triumphs, successes, accomplishments, and special events. You might say, "I'm the girl who won the race" or "I just got married" or "I was accepted into a program at a top college." These stories can also feature the negative things you have been through, such as illness, divorce, loss, and failure.

But remember, you have had many lives, and along with those lives come the stories you formulated at the time. The stories you told about yourself in a past life were true then, but you now have a different life, with unique stories. When you change your perception of reality to include all your past selves, you begin to realize that who you are is so much more than your story.

It is easy to get stuck in the story of this life, the one you are living now. After all, your story describes your daily reality an-

DIG DEEPER

I want you think about your story, the one you tell yourself and others about who you are and what you are all about.

As you bring this story to the front of your mind, notice how it makes you feel.

What role does this story play in your life?

Does the story change depending on who you are telling it to? If so, how?

chored in how you look, what you do, what has happened to you, etc. Who you would even *be* without your story? The key is to remember that your story is only one sliver of the much larger pie. You have thousands of stories that have spanned many centuries and across every continent.

History is essentially a story told by a society, through the lens of the elite and privileged, the rulers, and the victors. That said, the stories we tell do have an important purpose. The art of storytelling is nearly as ancient as time itself, and it's a fundamental part of being human. Stories share information in a way that plays to our empathy. They are how we can understand each other as individuals and the paths we have walked. We tell stories to make sense of the world and our place in it.

Our ancient ancestors painted in caves. These depictions of key events or accomplishments imparted practical knowledge and established beliefs about the culture. Over time, these stories evolved into oral traditions that were passed down from generation to generation and eventually became narratives that were spoken, performed, written, and typed.

Every culture on Earth has a storytelling tradition, whether it features myths about how the natural world works or legends about incredible feats performed by ancestors. These stories remind a group of their inherent greatness. Stories are how we establish the rules of a society and outline what is expected of us personally and collectively. Our stories reflect our values.

Stories such as fairy tales talk about mystical happenings that illuminate our spiritual beliefs. Through stories, we can be reminded that there is much more to our existence than what meets the eye and that anything is possible. In particular, myths are stories that deal with certain aspects of the human condition such as good and evil, why we suffer, the nature of life and death, the existence of an afterlife, and the presence of a deity or many deities. They shine a light on the beliefs, values, and everyday experiences of a particular civilization or culture. Think of the belief systems of ancient Greece, ancient Rome, the Norse or Vikings, and early Mesopotamia.

It is also through storytelling that we stay connected to our past, by recounting tales of what happened so we can learn from history. Such cautionary tales were designed to warn the listener not to repeat a mistake.

Sometimes, stories aim to influence beliefs or attitudes involving power and control, using the strength of storytelling and the emotional connection it brings to form negative ideas about specific individuals or groups. A clear example of this is the persecution of "witches" and the demonization of individuals who were healers, were midwives, or otherwise had ideas outside the mainstream.

Another example is the smear campaign against Friday the thirteenth as an "unlucky" day. This was a tactic employed by the early Christian Church to undermine the power of the divine feminine in the previously pagan society and establish a patriarchal belief system that would uphold the Church's power. Friday is connected to Freya, the Norse goddess of love and fertility, and the number thirteen indicates how many menstrual cycles women have in a year under the lunar calendar (not the solar calendar that the patriarchal system had introduced). Friday the thirteenth was considered an auspicious and sacred day in celebrating the divine feminine, the earth, natural cycles, sex, transformation, fertility, and womanhood.

Stories began to circulate about women who honored this holiday, accusing them of being witches, and the local powers even began holding executions on Friday the thirteenth to introduce the idea that bad things happen on that day. The story became so powerful that it still exists. Thus is the power of stories; telling one again and again often leads to it being accepted as truth, whether or not it has any merit.

A biography is a history of an individual told by another person as they see it. An autobiography, on the other hand, is told from the point of view of the storyteller themselves. It is a glimpse into the heart and the mind of the person who lived through the events in the tale, and even though it is considered

JOURNAL TIME

YOUR SOUL'S AUTOBIOGRAPHY

One of the ways to tell your story is to write an autobiography.

This is a version of the history of your life that is written and told by you, the person who lived it.

Spend some time creating a story from one of your past lives. It can be a real, remembered past life, or a fantasy that takes inspiration from a certain time period.

Write this story as an autobiography, as you either remember it or imagine that you experienced it.

Be sure to include details about who you were, what you wore, where you were, and what happened and why.

Also include the emotions you felt or imagine you might have felt—was it sad, scary, happy, strange, terrifying, or passionate?

What was it like to be there, in that past life?

less objective than a biography because it is undoubtedly colored by the attitudes and views of the storyteller, a first-person account adds emotion, life, and humanity.

When you begin to open yourself to all of your past lives, you realize that the story you have been telling, and have come to identify with, is simply not true. Or at least it isn't the whole truth because it only includes the details and circumstances of *this* life.

If your story is "I am a Clevelander," that doesn't factor in all of the other places where you have been born and lived. Perhaps you are also from France, Morocco, Bangladesh, and Japan. "I am a teacher" fails to include your previous professions and roles you have played over many lifetimes. Without all the details, your story isn't true because it is isn't complete. A story that captures everything would be a very, very long story!

In our past lives, we have gone on journeys to distant lands, sailed across oceans, witnessed turning points in history, fought and died in wars, had husbands and wives we loved and lost, raised children, made friends, built homes in different countries and places, had various jobs and professions, and much, much more.

For many of my clients, the stories and tales from their past lives become a part of their memories, which can be accessed anytime they like. As you unravel your past-life stories, those memories can become a part of your working memory bank. Maybe you lived a past life in Italy and now can recall enjoying

GET CREATIVE

Imagine that you are having dinner with some good friends after just returning from experiencing one of your past lives.

They are eager to hear about your adventures, and you are excited to share everything you did, ate, and drank; the people you met; and the sights you saw.

I want you to put together a presentation for these friends in whatever format you like, whether that's a slideshow with pictures, a drawing, a video, or any other creative way that allows you to share the story of your past life.

the scenery and food just as easily as you might think back to a vacation you took last summer.

Imagine if you could share photo albums and souvenirs of your travels with your loved ones and fill in the details of your adventures spanning centuries!

Because the story you tell is not who you are, it is not a solid foundation upon which to shape your identity. And because your story is not fixed, but rather shifts and changes over time, even apart from your various lives, constructing a sense of self around it is like building a house on a layer of quicksand. People move cities or countries, change jobs or retire, and get married or divorced. If you are too attached to one part of your identity, you can feel like the bottom is falling out of your world if that part shifts or evolves.

Maybe before you had children, your story—which was true at the time—was that you and your spouse were a young, working couple who were both trying to make their way in the world. After becoming parents, you needed a new story that reflected that enormous life change. When your children grew up and left home, you needed another story. Later, when you became grandparents, another story was needed.

Your story also alters over time as your perspective does. As you get older (or live more past lives), you gain experience, which helps you see things based on a new level of maturity. Something you considered vital at one point might have faded into the background as you got older. If you were to tell the story of how your kindergarten classmate bullied you, five-year-old you would have a different rendition ("She was mean to me!") than thirty-year-old you. Some of the details would remain the same, but older you hopefully would have a better understanding of the nuance and complexity involved.

It works the same way with your past lives. Looking back at something you did thousands of years ago and judging yourself for that behavior from today's lens of knowledge and wisdom isn't fair. We grow, we evolve, and we become wiser. That wisdom allows us to change the way we tell our story and the way we understand it.

I once worked with a woman who recalled being a man in sixteenth-century Venice, a wealthy merchant and philanderer. She saw that she had a wife, a woman who was gentle and kind, had "sad eyes," and reminded her a lot of her grandmother in this life.

But this man spent his nights in brothels—drinking, debauching with prostitutes, and living a decadent lifestyle he felt he deserved—with little to no regard for his wife. My client recalled becoming ill, likely from syphilis, and saw that his wife had developed the same symptoms. He watched his wife die, feeling regretful and guilty that his choices had impacted her in such a horrible way.

My twenty-first-century client was incredibly angry with herself for this behavior. How was it possible that she had been such a jerk to women in that life—not just his wife but also the prostitutes he had used?

I had to remind her that this man was her distant past, a former version of herself who hadn't yet learned and grown. She was a feminist, an activist who supported women's rights, and she regularly used her voice to speak out against misogyny.

She also was a loyal, loving spouse who had an honest, fulfilling relationship that she and her partner had chosen to make monogamous. Her grandmother, who she felt had been the wife she had betrayed, was one of her closest family members, and they enjoyed a deep, loving relationship.

Her current life reflected the evolution she had gained in the past five hundred years. I told her it was important not to judge herself for her past actions, but instead to look at the experience as an indicator of how far she had come. Instead of telling herself a story in which she was a terrible person, a bad partner, or a womanizer, her perspective as an older, wiser soul allowed for that story to expand to integrate her less-mature self with the kind, thoughtful person she has become today.

In a similar way, you can look at your own past lives as your inner kindergartner because they represent a version of yourself that no longer exists. We learn by doing, so to have gotten to where you are today, you had to have stumbled and fallen or failed to get it "right" many times before.

That is the point of reincarnation: to move us forward in our spiritual evolution and give us opportunities during many lifetimes to attain wisdom through our varied experiences. I believe that what matters the most is that you keep trying and remain committed to becoming the best version of yourself you can be, in each moment of each day.

Now, don't get me wrong. Your story is true on some level. The things that have happened to you, what you have done, where you have been, and who you have loved are all facts about you. But when you can open the curtains wider and see that you have many more stories, you can also see that you are much *more* than your story. When you can transcend your story, you are no longer limited by it.

Like the medicine woman taught me, when you realize that you are in control of the story you tell, that you can decide the details and even change the outcome, that story becomes old and outdated. The story that isn't serving you doesn't have to be the story you tell. When you stop telling it, it will stop following you around.

You can be free from your story. You can even choose to write a new story because you are no longer limited by the old one. There is power in the process of losing your story and realizing that you are so much more than the details and circumstances of this life. You can revise or rewrite it anytime you like. You are the author.

I once worked with a man who wanted to become a lawyer but failed the bar exam several times. He was down on himself and decided he would give up on his dream. Then he recalled a past life in which he had been a lawyer who failed to prosecute a murderer because a mistake he made led to a mistrial.

He immediately recognized this story, where he was a failure as a lawyer and unable to understand the due process involved with that career. When he saw that a past life was informing his current story, that it was a pattern that had carried over from a previous life, he realized that he was allowing the story to continue to be true.

He decided to double down and take the bar one more time. This time he passed and began working as a lawyer, realizing his longtime dream. His story wasn't serving him, and he no longer wanted it to be true. So he changed it to reflect the beliefs that he wanted to have about himself and his career.

Because you are not your story, you can rewrite it anytime you like and create a new one that reflects who you want to be. Knowing your past lives can help you realize that so much of your story is still yet unwritten and that you get to choose where it goes next.

And who knows how the story ends. You get to decide.

REVISIONIST HISTORY

REWRITE YOUR STORY

Get out your journal.

Imagine that you are stuck in an elevator with a stranger, someone whom you have never met.

The stranger has just asked you what your story is.

What do you tell them?

Write it down as it comes. Don't think too hard about it.

There's no need to embellish or edit. Just write what you would tell this stranger. Make it at least three or four sentences.

Who are you?

What has happened to you?

What roles do you play?

What is your job or purpose?

Include any details you like, whether negative or positive. Now, read the story back to yourself out loud.

Imagine that you are the stranger who is listening to this story.

What thoughts do you have about it?

Is it a good story or a bad story?

Do you make any judgments or assumptions about this stranger who is sharing their story with you?

Now I want you to ask yourself:

Who are you without this story?

What elements of this story don't need to be true?

What are you telling about yourself with this story?

Create the Future

nine

THE CYCLES OF BIRTH AND DEATH

The one thing we all can count on in life is that someday we are going to die. We know our current life will end and our human bodies will die. But death and what lies beyond remain the great unknowns for most of us.

As with anything unknowable, most of us have at least a few fears around the topic.

None of us can escape death. We experience the loss of our loved ones, sometimes tragically or unexpectedly. At other times, we watch people die slowly as their bodies succumb to illness, disease, or old age. Death is something we all think about because it is inevitable.

All things die, but the time, place, and means can't be known. We can only count on the fact that the moment will arrive; when and how are often out of our control. This helplessness only adds to the mystery and fear.

What happens after we die?

This question fascinated even our most ancient ancestors. There is significant proof that early humans believed in life after death, even reincarnation. They lived deeply connected to nature and saw the constant cycles of life, death, and rebirth around them as a part of their existence as well.

Our ancestors noticed that the sun disappeared in the evening, only to rise again in the morning. They noticed that the leaves changed colors and fell off the trees when the weather began to cool and the seasons changed from summer to autumn. Then, despite appearing to be dead or lifeless all winter, the trees sprouted new growth and the leaves came back in the spring. Because the people understood that every living thing is a part of nature, when someone died, it was reasonable to expect that they were part of that endless cycle as well.

We can gather quite a bit of information about how early people felt about death and what might happen afterward through archaeological finds that highlight rituals, habits, and daily life, as well as art.

A recent discovery of a Neanderthal burial site that is more than fifty thousand years old has revealed that this species had rituals for burying their dead, including placing the bodies of their loved ones into prepared graves with objects such as flowers, pollen, and tools. This find challenged the previously held notion that Neanderthals were unintelligent and unsophisticated. In fact, they thought about death and honored it as significant and meaningful.

Cave paintings up to thirty-five thousand years old have been found all over the world. Many show events that were a part of the daily life of the people who created them, including death. Some seem to depict a spirit, or soul, leaving the body of an animal at the moment of death. There are drawings of other-worldly beings, spirit animals, and renderings of an afterlife. Evidence also suggests that our early ancestors saw the caves themselves as portals to the afterlife.

As humanity evolved, each culture created rituals and customs based on these beliefs. Some of the most elaborate of these were found in ancient Egypt, where the dead were mummified so they could continue living after death. Important people and royalty were buried with all of their belongings, including their servants and wives, so they could come with them into the realm of spirit.

The Vikings, too, had elaborate funeral rituals, most famously funeral pyres, or large fires for the purpose of cremation. The idea was that the smoke and ash would rise and carry the spirit of the deceased into the afterlife. The funeral pyre is also part of the funeral ritual in Hindu traditions. Most cultures have traditions about washing and preparing a body after death and about what is said or done in the presence of a body.

The question of what happens after we die is, in many ways, the basis of spirituality and spiritual beliefs for nearly every society. In fact, the drive to question our existence and what lies beyond it is what makes us human and distinct from every other species.

Except for the few of us who have had direct experience with death, through near-death experiences (NDEs) or returning to life after experiencing clinical death, it remains an abiding mystery, with outsized influence over how we contemplate our existence.

THOUGHT-PROVOKING

What experiences have you had with death?

This includes the deaths of loved ones or family members, acquaintances, pets, or any other loss that comes to mind.

How have these events shaped how you think about death?

This fascination with life as we understand it (or not) doesn't just center around death; we also have questions, customs, and rituals around birth. Birth is every bit as mysterious. Most of us see birth as the beginning of life; we emerge from our mother's womb, and as we take our first breath, our life begins. Many people look at birth and death as bookends, with the life you live filling the space in between. They are a clear beginning and end.

Many wonder if, after we die, there is nothing but darkness, if our consciousness is gone. It can be painful to think about having to leave loved ones behind or giving up the life you worked so hard to build.

But what if that weren't true? What if death is not an ending? What if birth isn't a beginning? What if both are merely a continuation of an ongoing cycle of life, death, and rebirth that you have experienced again and again? What if you already have been born and died many times?

What if you are never really born and you never actually die?

One of the biggest shifts I see my clients make during our work together is their approach to and relationship with death.

JOURNAL TIME

I want you to imagine that you have just died, and you have been tasked with writing your own obituary.

What does your obituary say?

What were your accomplishments in life?

How do you want people to remember you?

What would you have done or changed about your life if you had more time?

When you have the experience of seeing yourself in a past life, in a different body and different form, you realize that your body is not who you are; that after a death, your journey continues.

I have seen many, many people remember dying in a different body, an experience that can change the entire way you look at death and birth.

People who have had near-death or clinical death experiences describe the event in remarkably similar ways, regardless of their background or spiritual beliefs. Because the components of an NDE are so congruent and do not seem to rely on any embedded beliefs or cultural expectations, many see them as proof of the existence of an afterlife.

The elements of an NDE, as described by survivors, include but are not limited to seeing a bright light; moving through what seems to be a tunnel; experiencing feelings of euphoria and peace; having a sensation of floating; viewing memories from your life rapidly flashing by; sensing a presence that feels loving and divine; and meeting and communicating with spiritual beings, including loved ones who have passed.

These are nearly identical to what I have witnessed many of my clients experience after they remember a previous death. When I am guiding someone through a past-life experience, I always have them go through the moment of their death and then, after that death, of leaving their body. I ask them to tell me how they feel, what it looks like where they are, and what else they become aware of in this state of "remembered death." Most describe the same light and tunnel, feeling calm, and being greeted by at least one spirit guide who was waiting for them on the other side.

Although no one has definitively proven the existence of the afterlife from a scientific perspective, research around the phenomenon of NDEs has opened many people to the possibility that not only is there a continued existence after we die, but that the experience is universal.

To me, if there is evidence of an afterlife, it makes sense that there would be a before life as well. Just like there are countless firsthand accounts of NDEs, there are many reports of people unearthing memories they believe are linked to past lives. Many of my clients describe having out-of-body experiences, either due to a traumatic event or while falling asleep. This leads to a realization that their body is separate from their consciousness because they can see their sleeping body while their conscious self, or their soul, is apart from it.

My clients also have past-life experiences in which they see that they are in a different body than the one they have now. They experience that life, with all of the emotions and memories associated with it, and then they recall their death. Even if the circumstances of the death are traumatic or violent, most describe the process of transitioning to spirit as peaceful. They feel no pain; only joy and love.

When you experience your past deaths, you lose your fear of death. That's not to say you want to die or be done with this current life, but the fear of the unknown is gone because you realize it is not the end, but rather a transition.

DIG DEEPER

What are some of your feelings about death?

Do you have any fears?

Take a few minutes to sit with this, contemplating your own death and the deaths of your loved ones.

Notice any emotions that arise. What are they?

Try not to avoid these feelings, but rather allow them to surface and observe them as they do.

Of course, no knowledge or belief in the afterlife can change the fact that grief is a very real part of life. Even those of us who have experienced death firsthand, through an NDE or a past-life experience, still feel the sorrow of loss. Approaching death via our many lives doesn't diminish the emotional process of letting go when we do experience it in our current lifetime.

We are emotional creatures, and attachment to others and to the beauty of life is completely natural. But having a more fluid understanding of death perhaps can change the way we grieve and let go.

Over the many years I have been coaching clients and working on past-life regression, I have had the honor and privilege of working with several individuals through their own death and transformation in this life.

Once I was working with a man who had terminal cancer. By exploring his past lives, he was able to see that there is a bigger picture to his existence and that his death would not be the end of his story. He was able to make peace with his impending transition as well as mindfully navigate how he decided to approach his relationships and ensure anything still left undone or unsaid was addressed. He passed away peacefully, knowing that his journey was much greater than this lifetime.

If you can realize that you have been born and died many times before, you can shift your relationship with death. This is true of your own death as well as the deaths of others. This change in perspective can ease your grief when you experience the loss of a loved one and also challenge how you think about your own death and even how you choose to live.

What if we were able to definitively know that death was not the end, but rather a transition into a birth or new beginning? How would that change the way we view the life we are living?

How would knowing that there is life before and after death, and that we continually reincarnate into new bodies, transform the way we make our choices about our current lives?

If we could collectively change our relationship with death by understanding that it is a transition and not an ending, perhaps we would approach life in a different way, too. Instead of spending time worrying about the details surrounding our death, we could more mindfully approach our lives through the lens of this knowing that where we are right now is based on all we have experienced and learned across many lifetimes.

Maybe we would even lose our fear of death completely, knowing that it is just a fear of the unknown.

Imagine that you have experienced memories from past lives that made you realize that you have died young more than once. How would this change whether you embrace becoming older, approaching middle age, and even stepping into your sage years? Receiving this knowledge might alter how you choose to use the time you have now.

Many spiritual traditions honor the idea of "death as an adviser for life," meaning that you can explore the fact that all living things die to give more meaning to your days and years. Perhaps we can approach our lives in a way that acknowledges the impermanence of it all while also giving us confidence in knowing that we are eternal and never truly die.

By changing our approach to birth and death, through understanding that we have lived before and died before, we also can become more empowered in our journey through many lifetimes. If we know that we are here, right now, for a reason and as one tiny part of an unending cycle, won't that impact how we view our purpose here?

Maybe we could even create a new future in which we all understand that we survive death and that we are far older and wiser than we ever knew. What if we approached ourselves with the knowledge that we are these wise beings who have witnessed, suffered, died, and been reborn?

What if we were able to look at others in this same way? Maybe we could create a future that honors this ancient wisdom, and by losing our fear of death, we could more completely and fully live.

MEDITATION MOMENT

Find a comfortable place to sit where you can have a few quiet moments to yourself.

Take a few deep breaths. Invite your mind to become still, and pull yourself into the present moment. Fill your entire chest cavity with deep, cleansing breaths. Feel yourself completely relax.

Now, as you continue to breathe, imagine that you have arrived at the moment of your death. Yes, it is time to leave your body.

Notice the emotions that arise:

What do you feel about having to leave right now? Fear? Worry? Sorrow?

Who or what would you miss? What is hard to let go of?

Now, ask yourself: What were the best parts of this life you just finished living?

What did you enjoy?

What were some of the things you regretted or wished you had done differently?

What did you learn in this life?

Allow yourself to immerse in the emotion of this experience. Really feel it.

You are in the process of letting go of this life and preparing to move on to the next one.

It's time to imagine your next life.

What body do you choose? What gender are you?

Where does this next life occur?

What would you like to choose or plan for your future, based on what you have learned in this life?

With whom do you want to reunite?

What new challenges will you give yourself?

Notice what comes up without judging it.

I want you to create a life plan for your next incarnation, complete with images of what it might look like, the way it might feel, and what you hope to accomplish.

Allow these thoughts to flow. With your plan in place—including who you will be, who you will meet, where you will be, and what you will learn and do—imagine that you are in a long, dark tunnel.

You can see a light at the other end, and you realize that you are about to be born again.

You slowly move toward this light, feeling a sense of anticipation and a knowing that you are about to be reborn.

Move into the light. What sensations do you feel around your birth?

Gently open your eyes and remind yourself that you can choose to be reborn again, right now, in this life.

What elements of the life plan you designed can you implement right now?

What did you learn about life from experiencing your own death and birth?

ten

CHANGING YOUR
POINT OF VIEW

By now, you have a lot of food for thought about your past lives and how knowing them can completely transform the way you think about yourself and your identity.

I hope the way you look at other people has also shifted, so you can see that who they are has nothing to do with their bodies or circumstances.

Because you are beginning to see how reincarnation works, you might even be in the process of transforming how you think about life.

So let's put it all together and figure out how to directly apply the knowledge you have of your past lives, and the principles about how reincarnation works, into your life today.

Yes, the past is fascinating, as is the study of history, but at the end of the day, life is what matters the most. Knowledge of the past is most valuable when it can teach us something about the present and where we are right now.

When you know the details of your own lives, you realize that you are not who you thought you were. Think of this change in perception like a trip to the optometrist. You sit in the chair, and the doctor checks your eyesight, placing different lenses in front of your eyes. With each lens, your vision alters, becoming sharper and sharper in focus until you discover the correct one, the one with the most clarity. In a similar way, past-life work can transform the way you look at everything.

You may never think about things in the same way again. I know I didn't. When I began to have past-life memories, my life transformed. I felt as if my eyes had opened to a completely new truth, and for me, there was a clear split between the time before I knew about my past lives and after.

The first thing that has happened is your shift in awareness. Now you know that you have lived before, in different bodies. The curtain has opened wider, and you can see that there is a much bigger picture to your existence. You have witnessed first-hand that you are not who you thought you were—your name, your looks, your ethnicity, your gender and sexuality, your thoughts or beliefs, your relationships and roles, your suffering, your story, and even your birth and your death.

Now that we have obliterated your previous conception of self, who are you?

It can be a lot to process. The first time I experienced a past life, it felt as if the mirror I had always looked into and depended on to reflect my sense of self had shattered. I was a man in that life, for one. I had experienced an entirely different lifetime, with its own triumphs and struggles, loss and pain, and at the end of that life, I saw myself die.

And after that death I had been reborn.

This information was a shock, and it took me a while to figure out what to do with it, to integrate it into a usable awareness, one that I could use to be happier; feel more fulfilled; and be a better, kinder, more loving person.

How can we use the knowledge of our past lives to change our life today? Once you know about your past lives, what do you do with them? How can you apply this understanding to your day-to-day, and what does it transmute for you?

REVISIONIST HISTORY

A NEW IDENTITY

How has what you have discovered about your past lives changed how you think about yourself?

Has it changed how you look at others?

Or life itself?

After this new information sinks in, and you have discovered all the past-life versions of yourself, it is time to integrate them and allow them to become a part of your identity.

The first thing to consider is that you are everything. You

are every expression of life, in every culture and every time period. Because you are everything, you are also none of those, or nothing.

When we place our identity on a false sense of self, or what some traditions call the ego, we are identifying with an illusion. This ego is the part of us that thought we were our bodies and our circumstances and has everything to do with living your current life.

Many people associate the ego with being self-centered, or a certain bravado or confidence, and it is true that overidentifying with the ego can lead to some of these attributes.

But remember, the ego is a false self. You don't need me to tell you this because you have experienced it yourself. You have seen your past lives and have witnessed the fallacy of identifying with who you are today.

Now, don't get me wrong—ego is what drives us to achieve, to partner with each other, to experience joy and pleasure. These are good things, and without them, life would feel more than a little dull and pointless.

Instead of allowing your ego to encompass your whole sense of self, though, let's expand the concept of who you are to include your prior selves, both your remembered past lives and the ones you have yet to remember. I'm asking you to reframe your point of view to include your past lives.

Keep in mind that you simply cannot replace your present-life identity with a past life. You can't just adopt a new name, a new cultural background, or another persona that represents a past life. That would be shifting from one ego identity to another.

Instead, I encourage you to see yourself as much bigger than one body or one lifetime. Begin to identify as the vastness of the universe and all the beauty it contains. Look at each other as the cosmos and Mother Nature embodied, here to do the work to become a better human being.

I have worked with many people who become moved, often to the point of tears, when they realize how meaningful and vast their existence is after having past-life experiences. There is often an immediate change to their confidence and the energy they exude when they realize they are a wise, eternal soul and not "just" a body.

You are boundless, everlasting, and infinite. So who are you to regard yourself as anything less than a miracle incarnate?

GET CREATIVE

Spend some time thinking about your own divine nature and the fact that you have lived many past lives and are part of a larger, infinite existence.

I want you to express this new identity as a piece of the cosmos creatively, as either a sketch or drawing, painting, photograph, flower and plant arrangement, rock or crystal art, or whatever you feel drawn to as a way to express the beauty that is you, the eternal part of you that continues to exist without a body.

Another change I have observed in many of my clients when they begin to see themselves as divine, eternal beings is that they become more intuitive. Many describe just "knowing" things; becoming more sensitive to energy or vibes around people and places; or having vivid, meaningful dreams.

I believe this is because they have remembered that they are tapped into a divine source. When they recall their true identity, they are able to use this power and source as a natural expression of who they really are.

Many of my clients have found that by uncovering memories from their past lives, they were able to step into their life purpose. This change in vantage point allowed them to realize not only who they are but also why they are here. Sometimes this purpose is connected to a career. Many change professions or jobs to suit their new perspective, based on what they now know.

I once worked with a woman who was at a crossroads in her career, having spent twenty-five years as a wife and a stay-at-home mother but now recently divorced and with an empty nest. She hadn't had a career outside the home in many years but needed to make an income in a way that was fulfilling and would allow her to share her gifts with the world.

She recalled a past life as an Impressionistic painter—work she truly enjoyed and was appreciated for. This experience allowed her to recall that when she was younger, her dream job was interior designer. By recalling this past life as an artist, she remembered her purpose and was able to start a successful business decorating homes.

Sometimes your life purpose doesn't come in the form of a job or career, but rather as a hobby or interest, or a role you choose to take on. I've had clients start taking music lessons;

decide to write a book; coach a kids' sports team; and take up hiking, biking, and enjoying the outdoors after remembering past lives connected to these activities.

I have also had clients pursue the healing or intuitive arts, learning reiki, psychic mediumship, shamanism, acupuncture, massage therapy, yoga, and, yes, even past-life regression, which delights me beyond words. One of the most fulfilling parts of my career (which is also my life purpose) has been watching my clients step further into the purpose they were born to share with others and bring joy and meaning to their lives.

Going back to my original question: After you discover that your identity includes all of your past lives, now what? Your identity and your point of view only change if you allow them to, so you need to figure out how to use that knowledge as a tool.

I often meet people who tell me they had an experience with past lives, through a regression, dreams, meditation, or spiritual journey work, but they don't know what it means.

My answer is always the same: Why don't you find out what it means?

You have to sit with it, think about it, understand and process it, and then use it to create the change you desire.

So what now? For one thing, your experience with your past lives can become your belief. It is one thing to believe in reincarnation and another to have experienced it yourself. That experience can become your own found, personal truth.

Also, by having these experiences, you allow your past lives to make their way out of the murky depths of your unconscious mind and into your conscious mind. Your conscious mind is the part of you that knows you are thinking and identifies with

MEDITATION MOMENT

Sitting in a comfortable position with your eyes closed, I want you to take several deep breaths.

And as you inhale, imagine that you are breathing in a beautiful light.

On each exhale, imagine that you are releasing any tension, worry, fear, stress, or negativity you might be carrying.

And now, as you become more and more relaxed, imagine that you have become a bird.

You can be any kind of bird you like, any species, as long as it has wings and is capable of flight.

As that bird, fly up and away from where you are sitting.

You can feel the sensation of flying, weightless in the air, and as you climb higher, look back and notice that you can still see where you are sitting, in meditation.

From this bird's-eye view, what do you notice?

What is your life like?

What perspective shift happens when you float above your life, your home, your family, your job, and your community?

your thoughts. And, as we have discussed, you are not your thoughts. When your past lives are embedded in your conscious mind, they can lead to new thought patterns and even new belief systems. Once you change your point of view, your behavior will change, and you will begin to make new choices.

Maybe before you began thinking about your past lives, you

tended to be hard on yourself about your body, your size, or your fitness level. After you incorporate your past lives, you realize that you have not always been lucky to have health and strength, so instead of dwelling on some ideal about the way you want to look, your focus shifts to a feeling of gratitude for your body.

Perhaps you are overwhelmed by your role as a parent, a spouse, or an employee. Remembering your past lives in which you didn't have family or a partner or you struggled to find employment will transform the way you look at these situations.

Maybe you have always maintained a certain stereotype about a person or a certain group of people, perhaps a specific culture, background, or race. When you realize that you have been part of that group or have been like those people whom you have demeaned, you realize that stereotypes do not fully capture the depth and breadth of their lived experience.

When you change your point of view, you look at everything through a new lens. You can see yourself as timeless, ancient. Maybe before you explored your past lives you hadn't considered yourself worldly or well-traveled, only to discover that you have already lived on and explored every continent.

Let me clarify that simply taking stock of your past lives is not the answer to all of life's questions. Rather, your past lives contain information about how you came to be at this point in your life and can guide you in your choices. People often come to me with big questions about where they are and want to know what they should do, but the answer is never simple. Maybe you are contemplating whether to stay in your marriage or get a divorce. You have a past-life memory that involves your spouse, who left you and caused you pain. That anecdote doesn't tell you whether or not you should leave *now*; it only tells you what the karmic story is, or the backstory to your relationship.

Perhaps remembering that past life makes you more committed to making your current marriage work. Alternatively, you could decide that leaving the marriage is the best way to bring things into karmic balance with your spouse. The past life doesn't tell you what choice to make; it only gives you a larger map to look at to decide which direction to go.

Your past lives not only are filled with valuable information about where you have been and why your life is unfolding in the way it is today, but also can contribute memories that are as vibrant as the ones you have from this life.

I love hearing people refer to their past-life memories with nostalgia, which means they are truly connected to those existences and the emotions that come with them. Our emotions make us human, so these feelings that emerge from our past lives are how we bring them home to have a place within us today.

Knowing your past lives can alter your chosen path and influence the choices you make by showing you where you have already walked, what you have enjoyed, and where you succeeded—and also illuminate what you might regret from your past and how you could have done better.

What you have learned from your past lives can lead you to an entirely new way of thinking that you can incorporate into your everyday life. Your past lives can become a part of your

DIG DEEPER

At this point, you more than likely have experienced several of your past lives and gotten a glimpse into your soul's history.

I want you to choose one of the past lives you have uncovered, even if it was a fleeting image or a thought, and focus on the person you were.

Imagine that you are sitting in a comfortable room with your past-life self, having a conversation.

You are relaxed and talking, sharing stories like old friends.

I want your past self to share a story with you about their life.

It can be a fact that comes to mind or a story you just made up. Let your imagination run free and create a tale from the life of your previous self that is worth sharing.

Maybe it surrounds an adventure they had, a challenge they overcame, a social or political issue that influenced their life, or a life-changing event such as falling in love.

As your past-life self tells this story, think about them as a wise elder, a grandparent or older neighbor who has stores of wisdom to share from a time before you were born, when the world was a different place.

After listening to their story, think about how that story compares to your own life.

How are your stories similar? How are they different?

And how did that story from the past change how you think about your life today?

identity, which features an understanding that you have lived before in many times and places. You are everything, but you are also none of that or nothing. You just are.

REVISIONIST HISTORY

This exercise should be done over the course of a few hours or even days as you go about your normal routine.

Notice when you have a reaction to a certain situation, especially if it is one that brings up strong feelings, negative or positive, such as frustration, anger, disdain, worry, satisfaction, pride, joy, etc.

Make a point to notice your emotional responses to the people and situations you encounter in everyday life.

And when you notice yourself responding to a thought or emotion, take a moment and stop what you are doing.

Catch yourself in that feeling.

What are you reacting to?

Are you frustrated because someone isn't doing what you expected them to do, whether it is a stranger or not?

Are you attached to an idea of "what is right" or "what should be or happen" in any given moment?

Turn the situation into a scenario in which you are in a past life, with a different body and circumstance but still experiencing this situation.

If there is another person involved, imagine that they have a different body, too.

What has changed about how you look at the situation?

Be sure to write down what happened and record your thoughts in your journal.

eleven

YOU ARE A SOUL; YOUR PURPOSE IS LOVE

We have been discussing what we are *not*: our name, looks, race or ethnicity, gender or sexuality, thoughts or beliefs, relationships or roles, suffering, story, and even our birth or death.

So . . . what are we then?

What is left for our identity?

The truth is that we cannot base our identity on anything impermanent, and all of the above features are fleeting, temporary, and, therefore, not the essence of who we really are. Uncovering memories from our past lives has helped us see this truth, that the circumstances of each and every lifetime are short-lived and in flux.

The only thing we can truly "be" must be permanent, enduring, immutable, and eternal, the part of us that survives death and reincarnates into a new body to experience other lifetimes.

This is your inner self, who you are without a body, and the essence to which you return again and again. It is your *soul*.

One of the ways I have come to understand the concept of a soul, or inner self, and how it can not only survive death but also change forms has been through the science of physics, specifically the first law of thermodynamics. This law states that energy cannot be created or destroyed but can be changed from one form to another.

We are essentially energy, so it makes sense that this would apply to us as well. We are not created or destroyed; we simply change forms. That transition happens at death and at birth over and over again.

Some people call this energy our consciousness, implying that there is an awareness of a sense of self that goes beyond our physical form. This term, *consciousness*, is used in the fields of psychology and neuroscience to contextualize how the brain works, specifically in terms of how we recognize, perceive, and understand knowledge, thoughts, and emotions through our individual senses. Your consciousness is your awareness of yourself and the world around you. It is unique to every individual. That means everyone has their own way of perceiving events, data, objects, memories, sensations, and feelings. We process it all through cognition, which is how our brain decodes what we are experiencing into a usable piece of information that allows us to achieve an understanding of what's going on around us.

Everyone has a different cognitive process, as well as cognitive strengths and weaknesses, so no two people perceive the same situation or object in exactly the same way. More than likely, you do not have the same brain or brain chemistry in every lifetime, which means that the way you perceive the world is not only unique to you, but also unique to your current existence.

There are debates within the scientific community about whether consciousness and cognition are a direct result of the brain at work because consciousness is a subjective experience and works differently for everyone. A robot can detect data such as color, texture, tone of voice, temperature, and so on, but consciousness describes the feelings and attitudes we have about what we have perceived. We are individuated on a neurological level, which is a more complicated process than simply brain waves doing their thing. Perhaps consciousness is not connected to cognition and is a separate process altogether.

There is no right way to think or be.

We can think of consciousness as an individual window to the world based on our varied experiences in our many past lives. Perhaps what gives us that one-of-a-kind filter came to us by way of our past lives. Our experiences are simultaneously universal, inherently human, and singular. Maybe what we call consciousness is a construct of being in a body, with a brain, and is only how we see things while we are incarnated. This consciousness is neither our body nor our circumstances, but it's also not our permanent "self."

Some people describe the eternal part of us as a "higher self" or "authentic self." I often call it our "Self" with a capital S, which differentiates it from the lowercase s self, which is how we see ourselves as a human on planet Earth. I like all these terms for different reasons. Authentic Self implies a genuineness that reflects our true nature and reminds us that our physical body and small *s* self is ultimately a false identity. The idea of a higher Self spotlights that elevated ideal and represents the better, wiser, more evolved part of who we are. You also may have heard it called a *spirit*, which not only allows for an afterlife but also lends a spiritual component that reminds us of how profound and meaningful our journey is. All that said, I prefer to call it a *soul*.

Our past-life bodies can't be who we are because they are dust. Our circumstances, stories, and relationships are fleeting and temporary. Once we let go, we can discover the part of us that is permanent. Uncovering memories from your past lives not only gives insight and perspective into the life you are living right now but also helps you discover the piece of yourself that you have always carried, the piece that has died and been reborn countless times.

By exploring your past lives, you can also discover your soul.

The ancient practice of finding ways to experience detachment from the physical self to discover your eternal nature has roots in nearly every culture on Earth. It has reached the mainstream by way of meditation, chanting, drumming, questioning your thoughts, breathwork, mantras, shamanic journey work, psychedelics and plant medicine, dreamwork, journaling, rituals such as lighting a candle, burning sacred smoke—and exploring your past lives.

These are just a few of the ways you can shift away from your thinking mind, or the part of you that identifies with the idea of the self being your body or your circumstances. When we find this nonattachment to our physical selves, we can become witnesses and observers and discover our true nature.

Our soul is our true identity and who we *really* are.

Shamans and healers from many cultures and backgrounds use a healing technique called "soul retrieval," which comes from the idea that when you experience something intense, often in childhood or past lives (or both), the emotions are an energy signature that you can carry after death and into the next life. If that experience is traumatic, sad, or troubling, it is possible to leave behind a piece of your soul.

Ancient healers knew that this splintering of your soul caused symptoms such as depression, anxiety, and addiction. They understood that any healing required for the body and the mind also was needed for the spirit because all three facets are intricately linked.

When you go back to that past experience, feel the emotions that come up, and allow them to rise from your unconscious mind, you are finding that lost piece of your soul and returning it to yourself. Once these shards are returned, and the wounding you experienced as that person has been examined, you can heal.

It did not take me long to figure out that this is what I was doing when I worked with my clients—allowing them to dive into their unconscious mind and retrieve parts of themselves they had abandoned, forgotten about, or denied, to become whole again.

The part of this process that always has felt profound is exactly how quickly the healing occurs, just by understanding that what you experienced was a past life. Even though the past life had been buried in your unconscious, its events still had an impact. This also suggests that without uncovering our past lives, we never can fully be healed or complete. These misplaced parts of ourselves are a part of a larger whole, and finding them can excavate our true identity to allow us to know who we really are: a soul and not a body.

When you embrace your past lives, you have a chance to get to know yourself on a deeper level. You can see that you are ancient and wise, that you have endured many challenges. You have a history that spans centuries, and you have lived and died in many ways.

Most importantly, you begin to have compassion for yourself. You see your own patterns, look at the lessons you have learned, and consider the challenges you have overcome. You can appreciate how far you have come, as a soul who has chosen to reincarnate in order to grow. This change in perspective also allows you to understand yourself as a soul that is still learning. Your soul is permanent, but it is also always evolving.

Years ago, one of my clients experienced a past life in which she had been what seemed like an early human. She recalled living in her cave with her wife and a new baby and had felt intense love for her family and an abiding desire to keep them safe. When a stranger happened upon her cave, his presence startled her so much that she reacted immediately and killed him with a spear. After, she cried and felt remorse for taking this man's life.

Looking back on this memory from tens or even hundreds of thousands of years ago, she realized now that he was probably just hungry and that she easily could have shared food with him.

I pointed out that since this experience, she has learned many lessons over many lifetimes that have shaped her into the person she is today—a kind and generous friend, who regularly volunteers at her local soup kitchen and is dedicated to helping people in need. She judged herself for something she did in the Stone Age, which would be akin to getting angry at a kindergartner for not knowing high school algebra. Through our work, she was able to see that over time she has become a kinder, more loving person, and she has developed compassion both for herself and for the process by which her soul has been learning.

The lessons we are here to learn in the school of life have to do with compassion, kindness, empathy, and ways to be of service to humanity. This is the "why" behind reincarnation. Your soul is here to learn how to love. In fact, love is our purpose and our mission. This includes self-love because we are challenged to establish better boundaries and put ourselves first when needed. It also is about learning to receive love.

When you track your past lives and get to know yourself on a soul level, you will be able to see that the reason you chose to reincarnate is to have the opportunity to give and receive love. Love is why we are here. Discovering your soul can help you realize this purpose and become more dedicated to carrying out this vital work.

There are many ways to love, and because we choose different relationships with our many soulmates during many lifetimes, we can explore all of its dimensions in human form. As I've said, you might have a daughter who was once your mother, a husband who was your brother or sister or friend. There is romantic love, familial love, friendship, and admiration.

We reincarnate to experience all of these versions and to learn from them. When you realize that you are a soul whose mission is love, that knowledge colors every interaction you have with others. It informs every decision you make, every thought you have, and every action you take.

When you understand that you are not your body, your circumstances, or the struggles you have endured, you start to see only the similarities among us. That's because the experience of being human is essentially the same everywhere.

TOOLS TO DEVELOP

HEART CHAKRA OPENING

Did you know it is possible to not only feel love but also experience it?

The heart chakra is the energy center through which we both give and receive love and how we share that love on a vibrational level with ourselves and others.

When we can learn to open our heart chakra, we have a chance to experience what love is like on an energetic level.

This love is not just limited to romantic love or the love we share with family and friends. The heart chakra is the source of a spiritual, divine love that is a love for all beings.

Are you excited? Let's give it a try.

Start by sitting comfortably and place both of your hands over your chest, right at your sternum.

Take several deep breaths. Begin by using your imagination to visualize that your hands are emanating a vibration that begins to move in a circular pattern.

As you sit, focus on this swirling, circular motion on your chest, just under your palms.

This energy is opening your heart chakra. Notice:

What sensations do you feel?

What do you see or feel behind your closed eyes?

Do any colors or patterns occur?

What emotions come up as you focus on this circular, swirling energy?

Spend as long as you like sitting here, using your hands to spin your heart open and allowing the energy that emanates to expand outward as much as you like.

You can do this heart chakra opening exercise as often as you like or as needed to feel connected to the energetic source of love that both surrounds us and is within us.

Discovering your soul can reveal to you that underneath each person's skin and the lives they were born into, in essence, we are all the same. We are all on the same journey, across many lifetimes, to learn and grow.

When you discover this truth, you can also see that the behavior and choices made by yourself and others are either as loving as they can possibly be or somehow lacking in love. This shift in perception takes countless lifetimes to master, so go easy on yourself. We are all doing the best we can and operating from where we are right now.

Love survives death. Over many lifetimes, we eventually can discover a love on a personal and on a collective level that lives in our soul. That love doesn't require anything of us because soul-level love just *is* and does not need to be earned.

Spiritual love is not an action or a doing, but rather a way of being. This is the love that can and will heal the world, and once you tap into that source, you will find that there is an endless supply in the universe.

When we connect to our soul or spirit, we uncover our true purpose, which is to love. That includes both the giving and the receiving of love. Many of us who have learned how to give love freely end up being martyrs or in codependent relationships or dynamics. Learning to accept love, and not in return for any kind of "doing," is a kind of love with a higher vibration. It just is.

Love is your purpose and your mission. Love and its lessons are why you chose to reincarnate and why you bothered to come back to Earth, in the body you chose and to the family you were born into. Love is why you have struggled, have suffered, and have overcome to get where you are today.

In fact, you *are* love.

MEDITATION MOMENT

Find a comfortable place to sit, and take a moment to ground yourself in your body.

Feel the surface you are sitting on. Place your hands on your thighs.

Take several deep breaths, filling your entire chest cavity.

Place both hands in the center of your chest, right over your heart chakra.

Notice what you feel—maybe a tingle or a vibration or a warmth.

Focus on someone who is close to you, someone you love deeply.

Send them an imaginary beam of light that comes out of your chest. It can be any color or combination of colors.

Watch them receive it. Notice how they feel from your light.

Think of all of the people you care about: your family, friends, coworkers, neighbors, and everyone who is a part of your life and you love and care for.

Send them a beam of light from your chest, and watch each one receive it.

Notice how it feels to be sending this light that is so filled with your love.

Now, send this same light to everyone in your city or town.

Most of these people are strangers, but they all are part of your community.

Send this light and love to all of them.

Now, expand this light to everyone in your country, regardless of where they live, who they are, or what they believe.

Send them this love light.

Be sure to include everyone, covering them all with this light that emanates from your chest.

Now, I want you to imagine that you are covering the entire planet and all living things with this beautiful light from your chest.

Send your love to all beings, and feel what it's like to have them receive it.

Now that you have sent out this light to everyone, everywhere, imagine that light is beaming back into your own chest.

That incredible, infinite light source of love is coming back to you.

Feel that light enter you and fill your entire being.

Notice what emotions arise and what it feels like to receive this beautiful light that is filled with a beautiful, pure, divine, spiritual love.

twelve

IT'S NOT WHO YOU ARE, BUT WHO YOU CAN BECOME

We human beings have an abiding fascination with the future. We want to know what is going to happen tomorrow, next week, next month, and next year.

We have been discussing past lives and how they impact us now, in the present. But does our past have anything to do with our future? How does it influence where we go next?

I believe that much of our fascination with the future and trying to suss out information about events that are yet to come stems from the same fear of the unknown that we discussed around death. We have an innate desire to feel in control and to quell our anxiety by knowing what to expect and predicting what is going to happen down the road.

But the future has not been determined.

We are constantly creating the future, based on our choices, so the future is actually something we can control. Your future is of your own making.

It is often said that if we want to know the future, we must first study the past. By examining history, we come to understand how it has shaped our reality today. We can evaluate how much has changed over time, notice the things that haven't evolved, and identify where we are stuck in the past.

History allows us to look at our past in both a critical and a constructive way to see where we have made mistakes, what has worked, and what has not. It can shine a light on the areas where we can do better, help us set goals moving forward, and allow us to carve a path toward the future we would like to have.

This is true for both our personal history and our collective, societal history. In many ways, your past lives are the key to understanding your own future as well as where we are going as a community, a country, and a part of humanity.

We have discovered that you are not a body but rather a soul. Your past-life history has taught you that you are not what has happened to you or any of the circumstances of your life. Your past lives have changed the way you look at who you are and have reshaped your identity.

You have also discovered the truth about the identity of others—that each individual on Earth is essentially the same: an eternal soul on a journey across many lifetimes, learning how to love and growing into a better human being.

Your past lives and past-life memories have revealed that any of your previously held thoughts or ideas that someone else is "other" based on their looks, gender, race, country of origin, language spoken, or economic status is simply not true.

That transformation in your point of view may generate a new belief system, which can and does impact the choices you

Think of a time when your attitudes impacted a choice you made.

If you had made a different choice, how would that have changed your future?

make. Those choices are forging your future based on your evolving attitudes and beliefs.

It is true that our desire to know the future so we can feel in control of our lives has created the widespread practice of finding ways we might obtain that information. It leads us to seek out individuals who we see as experts in the field of knowing what is to come, such as psychics and seers, as well as objects believed to prophesize. This practice of fortune-telling is an ancient one that can be traced back to every culture on Earth.

The most famous example of an ancient world psychic is the Oracle of Delphi, located at the Temple of Apollo on Mount Parnassus in Greece. Visitors to the Oracle would encounter the Pythia, the high priestess, and be invited into a question-and-answer session with her that would result in a prophecy or her take on the future of the person asking the question. The Oracle was in operation for nearly twelve hundred years, from the eighth century BCE until 393 CE, when the Christian emperor Theodosius I ordered all the pagan temples closed.

The Oracle and her prophecies were considered highly prestigious during this period and were mentioned extensively by writers such as Plutarch, Ovid, Sophocles, Plato, and Aristotle, to name just a few. Archaeologists now believe that the Oracle was located on a volcanic fissure, and the Pythia was having visions in an altered state of consciousness induced by inhaling the resulting gas emissions. (Don't try that at home.)

Using objects to tell the future, or divination, includes the practices of astrology, palmistry, numerology, and cartomancy, which is the use of cards such as tarot. Some cultures have practiced pyromancy, too, which is the use of fire to see the future; geomancy, or the use of marks and lines in dirt or rocks; and extispicy, which is the prophetic art of reading the entrails of animals.

Because the desire to know the future is ancient, so are these forms of divination. In fact, some are so ancient, it is virtually impossible to trace their origins.

Astrology is believed to have originated in Mesopotamia as early as the third millennium BCE. The I Ching, or "Book of Changes," is a system of symbols designed to find order in seemingly random events and a tool to predict the future that was written around 2800 BCE, almost 350 years before the construction of Khufu's Great Pyramid of Giza. The Norse people engaged in fortune-telling by reading runes, or rune stones. And the reading of tea leaves has been traced to ancient Greece, the Middle East, and Asia.

Our collective obsession with predicting the future is still very much alive. But the truth is that there is no *one* future to predict; the future changes in an instant because we always have choices available to us. Because we can make a new choice at any time, we have the power to change the future.

That means that even the most talented intuitive can predict a possible, or perhaps even a probable, future at best. We form the future with our choices, each minute of every day. There are infinite possibilities. Now, I am not knocking the practice of consulting psychics, but just know that no one can ever tell you with 100 percent accuracy what will happen.

You make the future with every thought, action, and deed. You alone decide what path to take.

It is true that some things do just happen. We can't stop natural disasters or cataclysmic events from occurring, and we cannot control the actions of others. Our present, as well as our future, can be directly impacted by the choices others make, too. But despite the fact that we may be helpless to things that present themselves in our lives, we can always choose how we respond to them.

One concept many of us associate with the idea of knowing the future is fate. This is the idea that the future is out of our control and is a fixed and, therefore, knowable entity. But the driving force that shapes our lives is not fate, but *destiny*. Destiny

DIG DEEPER

I want you to think back to a time when you took actions to avoid an outcome or consequence you found undesirable.

What did you do to change the future?

How did that experience change the way you look at your life or how your future unfolds?

Did you feel empowered to chart your own future through this experience?

captures the idea that we are active participants in our future and implies that there is a creative element to it because we can shape the events in our lives. Destiny also implies a higher purpose around those fork-in-the-road moments and that our choices enter us into a life that represents the quality of those decisions.

In fact, the word *destiny* means "to make firm or determine," such as in the word *destination*, which is a place that we end up at after plotting a course and determining where we would like to go. I also believe that destiny means to forge a future that represents the highest potential for yourself in this life.

Now that you know about your past lives, how does that change your future? How will this new knowledge and new identity influence the choices you make? How can knowing your past lives change your destiny?

There is a wonderful quote attributed to Carl Jung that says, "Until you make the unconscious conscious, it will direct your life and you will call it fate." This highlights exactly how your past lives can transform your future because even long before you became aware of your other lives, they existed in your unconscious. The unconscious mind is powerful in how it controls your thoughts and actions, so when you bring your past lives out of the shadows and make them conscious by remembering them, they are no longer the driving force behind the choices you make.

Imagine that you had a past life that featured a significant disappointment and heartbreak. Although it's not a part of the story of *this* life, you're still carrying around that heartbreak, which may be causing feelings of depression, hopelessness, and isolation from others, particularly potential love partners. Your past-life hurt keeps playing out without resolution.

When you recall that past life and see where the feelings of heartbreak are coming from, you understand that your sadness is not based in anything going on right now and you can change your behavior based on that knowledge—and perhaps open your heart to finding love.

Maybe then you meet someone. You nurture a beautiful connection that turns into a lifelong commitment that brings you peace and joy. By choosing to become open to love, and making your unconscious conscious, you can change your future and put yourself on an entirely new path.

Each of us is evolving and growing, slowly but surely becoming better, more loving versions of ourselves. As we can shift how we look at ourselves and others by realizing that we are all souls who have reincarnated in different bodies and forms, we also can shift our behavior. Knowing our past lives means that we can actualize a new future for ourselves, for our loved ones, and ultimately for our collective humanity.

I have said that if everyone, everywhere, really understood how reincarnation works, world peace would follow. If we all understood that we are not a body but rather a soul, we would be able to conceive a society of equality, understanding, acceptance, and love.

I know this is a lofty goal, especially because we are falling woefully short in these ideals. It often feels like all we see are acts of war, hate, prejudice, violence, and divisiveness. But I truly believe that exploring your past lives, and opening your mind and heart to the idea that we are all souls journeying through many lifetimes, is the first step in bringing this new world into being.

DREAMWORK

I want you to set an intention before you go to bed tonight to invite a dream that features a future version of yourself.

This you could be farther along in this life or in your next life. Ask your spirit guides, your higher self, or your unconscious mind—whatever source you like—for inspiration.

Then ask them to allow you to see a bit ahead, into the future. Record the experience:

What was happening?

What has changed from now?

What viewpoint does this glimpse into the future give you?

Do you like this future? Is it a future you would choose for yourself if you could?

If you don't like what you see, what do you need to change today to adjust your trajectory?

Your past lives have opened a window to yourself, your life, the people and events in your life, and the meaning and purpose of existence itself. We see that in our past lives we have all been victim and perpetrator yet also had moments of beauty and courage. We see ourselves as a soul. We see others as a soul. And we can make choices for ourselves and others that are more loving, more compassionate.

Now that you know *you* create the future, where do you want to go?

Who do you want to become?

When we uncover our past lives, we discover that we are so much more than we previously thought. We already have been old and wise many times, and when we recall our memories, that wisdom becomes usable today.

We can all decide to embrace the knowledge that life in physical form is about challenges, lessons, and growth, and we

JOURNAL TIME

Get out your journal.

Imagine a future version of yourself.

Maybe this you is many years in the future in this life, or maybe you can imagine that you are reincarnated in your next life.

Either way, discover a future you.

Write down who you have become.

What kind of person are you?

What do you contribute to the world?

Write a letter to your current self from this future self.

You can address yourself in any way you like, but the letter should focus on advice about what choices you should make to get to your future self.

Tell yourself how you got to where you are:

What did you do or fix or change? What did you need to let go of to become who you will become?

What did you need to allow into your life?

Be as detailed as you can.

can find peace in knowing that we chose it all because we want to become better. We decided to be here at this time on Earth. Yes, these times are challenging. But I believe that this era of our story as a human race is a pivotal one and that we are being called to step a bit further into our evolution.

You signed up to be a part of this, and you even volunteered to bring your earned wisdom to raise the consciousness of the planet. You were made for these times, and all your past lives and the previous versions of you have led you to this moment.

Embracing your new identity as an eternal, beautiful, divine, wise, and loving being who has decided to reincarnate as a human being for a little while can help you live that truth. Your newfound knowledge can nudge our collective trajectory toward a world of peace and understanding of our shared humanity. All your thoughts, actions, and deeds will ripple out and inspire others.

We don't have to wait until we die to reincarnate. Every day is a chance to be reborn. I am sure that many of you can relate to the idea of having a "past life" in this life because even looking back at your younger self, you can witness how much you have grown. It can seem like you don't even recognize that person.

As souls who are inhabiting a human body, our superpower lies in our ability to transform. We are never stuck or stagnant, but, like everything in nature, we are constantly moving through cycles of transformation. We are dying and being reborn, every day. It is important to remember that any change to our collective, or to the world we are creating, always begins with our own transformation.

And so, now that you know who you are—how will you reincarnate?

acknowledgments

I would like to begin by thanking the many incredible clients I have had the privilege of working with over the years. I am so grateful for the opportunity to witness your journey of healing, and it was truly an honor to hold space with you. Thank you for trusting me and for allowing me to learn from you. This book would not be possible without all of you.

To my agent extraordinaire, Laura Mazer. Thank you for seeing me, supporting me, and nurturing me through this process. I am eternally grateful for your wisdom, for your tenacity, and for your believing in both me and my message. I am blessed beyond measure to have you on my team.

And to my amazing editor, Nina Shield, and everyone at TarcherPerigee. I am so grateful for all of your guidance, thoughtful edits, creativity, and vision and for your helping me birth this book into being.

Words cannot express my gratitude to Dr. Brian L. Weiss and Carole Weiss. Thank you for opening the door for me onto an entirely new world, for showing me that there is magic that happens every day, and for your continued love and support over the years. And thank you to Amy E. Weiss for your endless encouragement; your friendship is so meaningful to me and I cherish it deeply.

I am so grateful for my "support staff," my parents, who have always been there with their support, even when they didn't always understand me.

To my best friend and soul sister, Jody, who is always there with solid advice and a grounded perspective.

And to my sister, Rebecca, my ride-or-die companion from day one. Thank you for continually challenging my point of view, for making me laugh like no one else can, and for your relentless love and fierce support.

To Jules, thank you for your constant support and encouragement, for being my mirror, my teacher. Your input, wisdom, and perspective not only helped me shape the message of this book but also helped me discover the person that I want to become. I am endlessly grateful for you and your presence in my life.

And last, but not least—to my children, Skyler and Jesse. Thank you for choosing me to be your mother, for helping me learn and grow, and for always loving me unconditionally. You both inspire me daily to become the best version of myself that I can be and bring me such joy. I love you both to the moon and back.